SUICIDE

IS NOT THE ANSWER

To Ms. Shavama
TooToo Thanks
for being so
Supa.

LARRY E. ROBERTS JR.

SUICIDE

IS NOT THE ANSWER

Suicide Is Not The Answer

ISBN 978-0-692-35339-4

Printed in The United States of America

FOREWORD

I watched Larry who struggled with suicide. He hovered dangerously close death. This victorious testament allows the reader to appreciate the bright light at the end of a dark tunnel.

In life, we experience the changing seasons and the times when life feels unbearable to the point that suicide appears as a way out. Larry shares the many seasons of life, and offers real time solutions for living...*Suicide Is Not The Answer* illustrates how we can move through the troubling seasons in Life

Pastor Hannah — New Life Covenant Church

CONTENTS

PREFACE

I, Larry E. Roberts Jr., am writing this book in hopes that it will inspire people not to end their own lives. After contemplating suicide, I decided I couldn't throw in the towel on my family, dreams and the things I'd worked so hard for. Life is what you make it, and you can't think that everyday is going to be filled with sunshine. There are going to be some cloudy days. How you deal with them determines how you will come out of your situation.

There's a saying that you have to go through in order to get to. Rome wasn't built in a day, and having something handed to you can be one of the worst things you could ever encounter. When you haven't earned something and it comes too easy, you won't know how to handle it, and you will take it for granted. There are a lot of youth today who have no morals and no values, and life means nothing to them. They are running rampant by shooting and killing one another, and they are not even sure why they are doing some of the things they're doing. They are going to jail for life at an early age, and this is really sad.

My desire is to be successful enough to show this new generation that there are other opportunities available for them. What people don't understand is we can have conferences and meet with our youth all day long, but until we can put those words into action, most of them just go back from where they came, and they will start doing the same things they were doing before they came to the conference. It is our job to implement things that can help them successfully make the necessary adjustments in their lives. There are no more Big Mamas. Babies are having babies, so grandmothers are not old anymore. They are in their late twenties or early thirties, which used to be unheard of.

That's why we need to hang around as long as possible, which the enemy doesn't want us to do. His job is to steal, kill and destroy. If I weren't trying to do anything productive, life would probably be a piece of cake. But because I am trying to do my part to help the world be a better place, it seems like my life has been a living hell. How could this be? The important things are to stay strong and know that the race is not given to the swift but to the one who endures until the end.

HISTORY

I was born on May 8, 1973 to Darlene M. Roberts and Larry Roberts, Sr. My father's parents were Andrew and Rosalie Roberts. My mother's parents were Harry and Patranella Lawrence. My mother, along with her other family members, attended Trinity All Nations Deliverance Church. The founder and pastor was Dr. Doris Evelyn Davis. Dr. Davis fell in love with Darlene at the age of twelve, and she asked my mother's mom if it would be OK if she stayed with her because she didn't have any children. Patranella was a little hesitant, but since the church was an upstanding one and Dr. Davis was an honest lady, she said it was OK. Larry started playing the organ and the piano at an early age, and Dr. Davis had heard him while visiting a church. Dr. Davis went over to Larry's home—he was only fourteen years old—and asked his mother, Rosalie, if it would be alright if he played at her church. He would be paid $25 a week. Larry couldn't believe it; that would be the most money he had ever earned. Needless to say, Rosalie said OK.

Larry started playing at Trinity All Nations Church where

he met Darlene. Larry told Darlene that she was going to be his wife. She told him that he was crazy and that would never happen. However, at the age of nineteen, the two married. Soon after marriage, I, Larry E. Roberts Jr. was conceived. This is the beginning of my life story.

CHAPTER 1

HOW IT ALL BEGAN

I was a witty, aggressive baby. During my mother's pregnancy, my dad put his hands on my mother's stomach and said that I was going to be just like him. I was a very active very friendly baby. When I turned two, my parents had another little boy and his name was Jermaine. I was told he was also a very happy baby. Unfortunately, Jermaine died at age one of crib death. That same year, a baby girl by the name of Tramaine was conceived. Larry and Darlene loved their two children. They always took us to church and did nice things for us.

It was unusual for my parents to allow us to stay over anybody's house, but there were some people who my parents began to trust, and I was allowed to spend the night at their home. There was a teenager in the home who appeared to be very nice or so I thought. I was only three years old when I started spending nights at the home of my parents' friends. They took a strong liking to me. Their teenage son grew very fond of me, and he never had a problem babysitting me. He babysat me along with his younger brother, who was my age. We were all one big happy family. We all went to the same church, and I often went out of town with them. What more could a kid ask for?

Even though I was too young to realize what was going on, I felt loved.

As time went on, the teenager always kept me physically closer to him than he did his younger brother. I was too young to realize what was going on. I just felt loved and taken care of. The teenager started taking me into the bathroom with him but that only happened when his parents weren't home. He made to play with his penis. I was a baby. I didn't realize I was being hurt. I did what I was instructed to do. Lastly, I was too young to convey what was really happening to me.

The more I went over to the home of my parents' friends, they more comfortable my parents felt leaving me there. My parents had no idea what this friend's teenager was doing to me. The more I went to their home, the more their son would fondle me and make me do things to him that were totally disgraceful. I turned four years old, and it continued to happen until I was five. I started being more aware of what was going on, but I didn't know that I was being abused or that it was wrong.

I was more aware, and I was also talking more, which meant I could convey my experiences to others. This also meant I had to be coaxed by my abuser into not mentioning what went on inside of the home of my parents' friends. It began to get worse. I was made to get completely naked and lay next to this boy who was also completely naked. He rubbed his private parts all up against me and made me do the same to him. At this time, he had to have been at least sixteen or seventeen years old. He was completely aware of what he had been doing, and he didn't care. He carried on these acts every time we were alone. No one was suspicious because I kept silent and there was no evidence that anything inappropriate had taken place. The abuse continued until I was five.

I couldn't say anything to his parents or my parents – besides, as a child, how could I explain something that I didn't know was wrong? If I said anything, I would be threatened or punished, which meant he would slap me around or punch me in my chest really hard. Being punched at five years old by a teenager hurt pretty badly. For that reason, I never told anyone because I knew what would happen if he found out. Adults rarely believed what kids told them because kids were known to make things up. My mom and dad always told me if anybody ever did anything to harm me, I should let them know, but I didn't know that what he was doing to me was wrong. I didn't know that there was anything to tell. I was also told that if I told people what he had done to me, they wouldn't believe me, and I would get in trouble for lying. Wow, I felt stuck! I just had to forget it ever happened. The molestation eventually stopped after he graduated from high school and went into the military. After that, he rarely came home, which gave me the opportunity to get older and wiser. The only problem was when I started getting older (from age eight to eleven), I started looking for the same feeling I had obtained as a result of being with this almost-adult teenager.

I had a very strong man for a father and a lot of strong uncles and male figures around me. Being a boy and liking other boys wasn't ever an issue for me. I knew that boys and girls belonged together, not boys and boys or girls and girls. So every time I went around girls, I always wanted to try what I learned. Little did I know they didn't really know any better either. They were looking to explore and experiment with their bodies. I found myself always visiting people's homes with my parents and wanting to go downstairs or into another room and "play house" with the girls. I really wanted to fast-forward to the kissing and laying in the bed part; the other part of playing house really didn't matter to me. What was happening to Little Larry, as I was affectionately called? Luckily no one ever knew, because we kids never talked about our secret.

My parents were very strict, but not to the degree where it was unbearable. They were really overprotective. A lot of their teachings came from the church of my grandmother, Dr. Davis. There were a lot of rules. Ladies were not suppose to wear pants, braids, makeup, long nails or nail polish. They were not allowed to cut their hair or do anything that made them look like Jezebels, which is how the church referred to these type of women. The girls were told not to take gym in school because it was also a sin to wear shorts. The men could not wear afros, neck or arm jewelry. We were taught absolutely not to ever question our parents or other adults when they gave us instructions. My sister, Tramaine, did whatever she was told to do, but I questioned everything I had an issue with. I may have gotten yelled at, but I needed to know why. How could I be a young person and could not do the normal things kids do? We were taught it was a sin to go to the movies, bowl, and play sports—pretty much anything that was considered "sitting in the seat of the scornful," as they called it.

I lived in a suburb where kids would ride their bikes to school, but I couldn't. I wanted to go outside, but my mom would say, "Stay in your room and read a book." I thought, "Man, I can't do anything!" I could do nothing besides go to church four to five times a week, go to school and do whatever else my parents saw fit for me to do.

My father, on the other hand, disagreed with certain things and decided that he wasn't going to stop me from being an athlete, playing sports, and being a young man. My mother was just overprotective, but she meant well. Having girlfriends was definitely out of the question, especially as far as my mother was concerned.

My dad became one of the most popular musicians and songwriters to come out of Chicago. Every time popular singers came to town, they would call my dad to play for them. By the late '70's, he was playing for everybody. He played for Albertina Walker, Milton Brunson, James Cleveland and many, many others. Some of his hit songs were "I Love Jesus," "Are You Ready?," "I'll Fly Away," and "Oh, Taste and See." He played on many records and performed on many television and radio broadcasts. It was a dream come true. I had the opportunity to meet so many great people. My dad had the opportunity to go and play for Motown, but he made a conscious decision not to go, for the sake of his family. There were things he could have possibly become involved in that could have easily dismantled his family. So my dad continued working for Royal Crown Cola. He decided to open up a restaurant and named it after him and my mom, D & L Bar-b-que. My dad is a great cook, and people would come from far and near to 107th and State Street in Chicago to eat his barbecue and fried chicken.

CHAPTER 2

MOVING TO THE SUBURBS

Being born and raised in the city of Chicago was great, as far as I was concerned. My father continued working for Royal Crown Cola driving a truck. During the mid- '70s to mid-'80s, the unions were very strong. He was able to make a lot of money. So, in addition to the restaurant, my mom and dad were doing very well for a young couple. I was twelve years old and knew how to barbecue ribs on the grill while I was up on a stool on my knees. It was a dream come true. I was working with my dad. He was my hero; so I wanted to do everything he did. My dad taught me how to make homemade barbecue sauce and pizza. I pretty much knew how to do anything in the restaurant that he knew how to do.

There was a lady who cut our hair, and she did a very good job. Times became very tight for my dad, so we couldn't get over to the barbershop as often as we could before. Needless to say, we had to find somewhere closer and more convenient, which ended up being a place right around the corner from my dad's restaurant. I could walk over to the barbershop on my own. Every time I went to the barbershop, I always asked the barber a million questions about cutting hair, not really thinking anything serious of it.

Eventually, my mom and dad decided to build a home in Matteson, Illinois. "I am ruined!" I thought. I am moving out to the suburbs away from the people I'm comfortable with. Plus, I was going to be going to school with people who were another color. Not only that, my dad decided to change the name of the restaurant to Larry's Ribs, and he found a new location for the restaurant in Matteson. I was not used to this, so I was not having it. I had to move out to the suburbs and there were no black barbers around, no alleys to play basketball or hide-and-go-seek and no one sat on the front porch in the neighborhood while we played rock teacher.

Living in the city meant that if you found something walking down the street, it was considered yours. In the suburbs, kids drop what their doing and run home for dinner. I was not aware of this, so I found a bike, bat, baseball, and a glove, and I ran home and told my parents. My dad told me to take it back because the kids leave their things sitting outside and no one steals them. I was disappointed, but I took everything back where I found them. I did not want to go live out there and go to school. I wanted to go live with my Grandma Lawrence (as we called her) in the city. My father's mom and dad also lived in the city, but there was not as much going on at their house like there was at at my maternal grandmother's house. My Granddad Harry had passed, so all of my mother's sisters and brothers lived with my grandmother. This meant that there were a lot of kids over there for me to play with everyday. We never had to go out and get other kids to play with. I had so many cousins, we always had complete football, basketball, and baseball teams. My Uncle Smiley was a great influence in our lives because he taught us how to swim and ride bikes. He also taught us street knowledge. If we were disobedient, he wouldn't let us go outside to play, but he would make us sit in the house while he watched the news and read the Chicago Defender newspaper. Our best bet was not to get in trouble. This is where I found my balance.

At home, my mom and dad were sanctified or considered "holier-than-thou," as people called it. My mother's side of the family knew that my sister and I were very bound, so they would always let us do things that we weren't allowed to do, such as go to the movies, park or walk to the laundromat. They would let us take the bus and the train. "What a wonderful life!" I thought. I was blessed to have parents who had cars and all the amenities needed for a family; so I enjoyed the many different aspects of life.

I was confused at this point. At home with my mom and dad, I had a lot of do's and don'ts, but at my Grandma Lawrence's house, I was free to be myself with only a few guidelines. The plan was not to tell my mom what we were doing at our grandmother's house because she would send instructions on what we couldn't do. We couldn't dance because it was a sin. We also weren't allowed to sing secular music. If we did these things, we were told we were going straight to hell!

The thought of going to hell where the fire was said to be really hot was out of the question. So I tried my best to live my life the way we were taught to in church. I was told that I would be blessed if I did, but if I lived any other way, I wouldn't be blessed. I had a lot of morals and values. There were things that no one had to teach me because my common sense kicked in. Therefore, I didn't use foul language, sing secular music, dance, drink, smoke, use drugs, party, or do anything we were told not to do. How hard could this be, especially since my peers were enjoying their young lives? I wanted to be blessed as I got older, so I didn't care what they did. I grew up believing that I had to live a perfect life, so of course, people around me were offended because it appeared as if I was judgmental, and they felt as though I thought I was better than everyone else because I could do no wrong. This was a hard battle to fight. But who cared? I was going to be blessed because I was doing everything in my power to live a perfect life. I almost forgot for a moment that I was not only a growing kid, but I was a human being. This meant that when my imperfections presented themselves, I had to hide them because I was a preacher's kid, and I didn't want to let my family down. Also, my peers would think I was a phony. I portrayed a perfect do-no-wrong life, and I judged them because no one could know the truth. I was also struggling with molestation. I had stopped thinking about it, but it came out in other forms and fashions.

There was a lot of wrong I was bound to do, but I was just not aware of it. I liked girls, and I became very promiscuous.

I was willing to go to any degree to get a girl. My mom didn't allow me to talk on the phone to girls, and I couldn't go and see them. Every time I asked to call a girl, my mom would always ask me, "Didn't you talk to her at school?" I had to sneak to call and see girls. I would go to church early enough to sneak outside and walk to the store to meet a girl so that we could kiss and hug.

I thought, "How lucky could I be?" I had my encounter to look forward to every Friday night before church started. Then it got worse. The feelings started getting even stronger, and I couldn't talk to anyone about it because we were instructed not to question why we couldn't do something we were told not to do. Needless to say, I was afraid to go to my parents and talk to them, so I just kept my feelings inside and did what I felt was best.

I learned a valuable lesson about not talking to my father. I was working at the restaurant one day and made the mistake of talking to another man who worked there about a problem I had. The man felt obligated to tell my father, and my father was very upset because he said that the door was always open for me to talk to him, and after that point, I went to him about any problem I had. I was a musician at my grandmother's church and I played the organ and the drums. I would talk to the girls before church that week, and we would plan how and when we were going to meet. The girls were just as bound as I was, which meant they were just as frantic as I was to fulfill these feelings.

The girls couldn't wear pants, which meant they always had on dresses or skirts. For me, that meant easy access. So while church would be going on, a girl and I (of course, it would be a different girl at different times) would meet in the basement of the church in the stairwell, and we would do our best to have sex. There was a bathroom for those with a handicap upstairs next to the inside of the church that I even had nerve enough to have sex in while service was going on. As a kid who was trying to express certain feelings, I was taught, I didn't think about how disgraceful my actions were at the time. All I could think about is the fact that at home it was very strict, so I had to express myself wherever I could. I was a very sneaky person, so I made sure I did everything in my power not to get caught, which I never did. If I would have gotten caught, I may not have lived to tell my story.

CHAPTER 3

TAKING CHARGE
OF THE SITUATION

I turned thirteen, and I felt led to put my energy to use in some other areas. I hated to lose at anything and always had to be the best at everything. We were taught to live perfect lives, so why wouldn't I try and be perfect at everything I did? I could play every sport and wanted to be the best at them all. If I didn't reach that goal, I would get very upset and throw a temper tantrum.

I decided to go to Walgreens and buy a $19 pair of clippers. This was my decision because I was all the way out in the country (as people described it), and I couldn't easily get to a barbershop to get a haircut. I came home and began to rant and rave over these clippers and how I was going to cut my hair and start cutting everyone else's hair, and I would be the best. I attempted to go into the bathroom to cut my hair, but my mother was not having it. She made me go into the basement.

I pleaded with her, and I said, "Mom how can I cut my hair downstairs without a mirror?"

She merely said she didn't care, but I was not getting ready to mess up her bathroom by getting hair everywhere. I didn't have a choice. I had to try and cut my hair in the basement using a hand mirror and unable to see behind me. How do I get a perfect haircut and I couldn't see what I was doing? I begged my mother to let me finish my hair in the bathroom. I told her I wouldn't make a mess, but she said no. My father stepped in and told my mother it was OK, and he would make sure I didn't make a mess. I did such a good job of cutting my hair, they couldn't believe it. From that point, I made the decision that when I got older, I would become a tonsure artist (barber stylist).

I started spreading the word in the neighborhood and around school that I cut hair, and I would be charging $3. My sales pitch was to tell a potential client that if he let me cut his hair and I messed it up, I would in turn pay him $3. If, however, I didn't mess up, the person had to pay for the services. Believe it or not, I never had to pay anyone. I was on to something very big. I was thirteen years old, and I made my own money. I made money as a musician at church, cutting hair, and my dad would pay me from time to time for working in the restaurant. I was in heaven. Nothing could stop me now, or so I thought.

As time progressed, the more I cut hair, the better I became and the more clients I had. Before you knew it, I started taking the activity bus after school to nearby communities and cutting hair in those areas, as well as my neighborhood in Matteson. My mom and dad saw that I was very serious about my craft, so they became very understanding about my having to travel to different communities to cut hair. Besides this was an opportunity for me to see girls outside of church or at family gatherings. I used cutting hair as my excuse for doing everything I wanted to do. When I would get on the activity bus after school, things escalated. I went to three different girls' homes on the same day and had sex with them. This was bad behavior. I was too young to be carrying on in this manner, but I never felt like it was a problem. These sexual encounters continued three or four times a week.

I was at home cutting grass after school on my sixteenth birthday, and my dad came home from the restaurant and told me we were going to get my driver's license. I could not believe it! I was actually going to be driving solo! What a dream come true! Then to top it off, my dad let me get on the high school basketball team. My mom was out of town on this day, and I had to go to church to play the organ for service. My dad allowed me to drive my sister and me to church. I couldn't believe all of these good things were happening to me in one day. On Monday and Friday nights, all of the kids and teenagers were forced to get on the alter to get saved, as it was called. Some of the parents went as far as beating their teenagers with a belt if they didn't want to get on the alter.

I would sit there when they told the teenagers to get up because I felt as if I had it all together. My grandmother would tell me, "I said get up here buckethead!" so I did. We had to lift our hands and pray and ask God to forgive us of all of our sins, and we would have to stay on the alter until the grownups felt as though we were free from sin. I would get tired of being on the alter, so I would look around to see if anyone was watching me. If they were not looking at me, I would take spit and wipe it down both sides of my face to make it seem as if I was crying. When the adults saw this, they would let me sit down because they felt like I was sincerely free from my sins. This went on for most of my teenage life, and it was an uncomfortable feeling.

On a particular night when I drove to church, my grandmother requested for the musicians to play a song. We were young, so we wanted to do a more up-tempo song, but she wanted a slow boring song. I didn't want to play it, so while church service was going on, she told her nurse to go up to her office and get her extension cord off of her coffeepot. She came over to the piano in front of everyone and told me that if I didn't play the song, she was going to beat me right there. I told her I was going to tell my father, and she said she would beat him, too!

I jumped up and ran outside until service was over, and of course, she later told my parents. My mom made it home that night, and when my sister and I got home she asked, "How did you guys get here?"

I replied, "In the car."

She asked, "With who?"

I said, "I drove."

She replied, "I'm going to tell your daddy I don't want you driving."

"He got his license," my dad said. "He can drive."

When I look back over that period, I simply view the situation as my elders trying to protect me from the hurt and danger that the streets had to offer. In retrospect, I was still confused because I felt as though I was missing something in my life as a teenager. I decided I wanted to run away because I hated the strict rules and living in the suburbs was the pits. I felt as though everyone was prejudice, and I wanted to go to the city and live with my Grandma Lawrence where I knew I could be a normal teenager. My mom called my dad and he rushed home and came looking for me. I was headed up the walkway with a brown paper bag, and he jumped out of the car and ran after me. I started running up the crosswalk, and my bag tore. Needless to say, my father caught me, but he persuaded people to think that he caught up with me and that his age at the time didn't matter. I just let him go on thinking, that, but the truth was, my bag tore. I went back home and had to explain myself; however, they were the parents I was the kid so no matter what I said, I still had to be obedient to my parents. I felt like I couldn't do anything at all. I was not like the normal kids. They were able to ride their bikes to school, but I couldn't. They were able to go outside whenever they wanted, but I had to stay in and read a book. They could go to the school functions, and I wasn't allowed to.

Tramaine, on the other hand, was content with living the way she was told, but I just wasn't having it. By this time I'm cutting a lot of hair, and I had really gotten even better. I was a full-time musician at church and performed four to five times each week. My father had gotten hurt on the truck at work, so he had stopped working at Royal Crown Cola and became a full-time musician and restaurant owner. He hired people who were robbing him blind. Not only would they try to steal money, they also gave away free food and threw boxes of meat in the dumpster in back of the restaurant and have their family members later come and pick them up. It was very hard to find good honest help and dependable people to work at the restaurant, so I took on a lot of responsibility. I would ride my bike over to the restaurant at 6 or 7 a.m., and I would get everything prepared. I would make barbecue sauce from scratch, light the pit, turn on the steam table, turn on fryers, make coleslaw from scratch, make homemade hotlinks, clean the ribs and the other meats, and I would have everything prepped to make sure the restaurant was ready to open. I barbecued ribs just as well as my father and my uncle with the fire in the pit blazing. I would work a full day at the restaurant, then I would go home and cut hair. Still, I tried to find time to play the sports I enjoyed outside.

I also had to get ready to go to church. I was a hard worker, and I figured all of this would pay off in the long run. All I could think about is becoming an adult, because in all of this, I still could not find a balance in my life. By the time I turned seventeen, I had to concentrate on graduating from high school, along with preparing for my career in barbering. I was "the man" at this point, because I was cutting everyone's hair. I couldn't be stopped.

My dad called me at home one day and told me to write a number down. I asked, "What is this? He said, "It is your private line I had it put in when I had the house built." Wow!!! I could not believe it, my own telephone line. My mother still tried to control my phone calls, but I had to tell her that I paid the phone bill, so I could really stay on the phone long as I wanted to and could talk on the phone to whomever I wanted. I ended up setting up a barbershop inside my basement at my parents' home, and I had so many clients that I had to get one of my friends to come over on certain days to help me cut hair. We would split all of the profits down the middle. By this time, I was charging $5 a head. I kept $200 to $300 in my pocket weekly from doing haircuts.

There was a young lady I was seeing who lived down the street from my grandmother's church. She said she couldn't get pregnant, so I slept with her one time, but that's all it took. While I was at church on the organ one night, my grandmother was dismissing service and told me she wanted to see me in her office. I didn't think much of it, so I walked in the office and this girl was sitting in the office with her family and my mom because my dad was at the restaurant. She said she was five months pregnant, and I was the father.

How could this be? She told me she couldn't get pregnant. So I was going out like that. I lied and said that I was with her as well as two other guys, so we didn't know whose baby it was. After I got over the embarrassment and humiliation, I decided to talk to my dad about it and take responsibility. My dad was very proud that I stepped up to the plate, but my mom refused to believe it had anything to do with me. I was her little boy. I was a church boy, so I was perfect, in her mind. When the baby was born, I told my dad I was going to have a blood test, and if it was my child, I would have to take responsibility for it. He said that was fine, so we will talk to her family about the situation. Her family members said it would be over their dead bodies that there would be a blood test, and I just had to take care of the baby.

I wasn't stupid. I knew I had only been with this girl once, and it wasn't until five months later that she said she was pregnant. That was the end of that as far as I was concerned, but there hadn't been a day that passed when I didn't think about this innocent little baby who could potentially be mine. Her aunt adopted the baby girl after she was born, and they moved away to another state. On with my life, I figured.

At the age of seventeen, I started barber school. I couldn't believe I was in barber school.

Everyday I left high school and went straight to barber school because my dad would let me drive on a regular basis. People said we were rich because we drove nice cars, lived in a nice house and owned our own business. They call my dad the Rib King and called me "Lil Rib Jr.

"I wore suits to school almost every day, or if it wasn't a suit, I had every basketball team warm-up suit with gymshoes to match. Not to mention, instead of carrying a regular book bag, I carried a Gucci, Fendi, or Louis Vuitton portfolio. I wore cologne, even if I just went to the park to play basketball, and needless to say, I was always voted best dressed every year I was in school. While at barber school, I maintained the same persona that caused what I thought was the administration to pick on me. I often took food from my dad's restaurant to everyone during the week, and I drove a nice car. People assumed I was spoiled. That kind of upset me. I knew how hard I worked on a daily basis, and I knew that I earned my own money, which allowed me to buy whatever I wanted.

This assumption often caused me to lash out. I felt I needed to protect myself and prove that I was tough in spite of being perceived as the "church boy/spoiled kid" with everything. I was already a good barber before I started barber school, so I never had a learning curve. I was cutting hair from the time I got to school, for the most part—until the time I left.

My skills permitted less people from getting their hair messed up by the newer barbers. I felt as though I needed to have a complete theory behind mastering the barbering techniques, so I had a bit of an issue with this. I was too outspoken, which always caused me to be threatened with suspension or even kicked out of the school.

I paid my way own through barber school. I didn't want to throw away my money, so I did my best at being a good student. I felt like fair was fair and I wasn't going to allow the barber school administration to just do me any kind of way.

I turned eighteen and graduated in 1991. My dad kept telling me on graduation day, "I got a surprise for you! I got a surprise for you!" I couldn't imagine what it could have been, so I didn't really put much thought into it. After graduation was over, we all met at my dad's restaurant in Matteson, and we were sitting down inside. My mom said, "Larry, what is that outside?"

I went outside and my dad pulled up in a 1991 four-door Blazer with a bow rapped around it. He got out and threw the keys to me and said congratulations. This was, by far, the greatest day of my life. What more could I ask for? This was one of the most popular SUVs on the market at the time.

People assumed I was. My father had bought me a new Blazer. People realized that I had graduated on Friday. But what they didn't know was that on the following Monday, my father took me to the car dealership, and I had to put my own deposit down for my car as well as pay every monthly payment. My dad knew that I was responsible, which in turn, he knew I could handle the upkeep of my own car, and he was willing to put his neck on the line for me. I really caught hell at barber school because my new car just sealed the deal of how spoiled they thought I was.

I started feeling as though I was ready to establish my own credit and pretty much prepare to be able to live life on my own.

I went searching for a job because I felt like working for my dad really didn't do me justice. Even though I worked as hard if not harder and more hours than some of the employees, I didn't get a regular check that would have made me worthy of proving employment to obtain a credit card. I found a job at Chemical Bank where I became one of the best telemarketers on the job. I later got my first credit card, and boy did I have a rude awakening coming. There was a shop where I worked when I was eighteen, and I would have people lined up from wall to wall waiting on me to cut their hair. I had everything going for me, but there were still some things I was missing. The most important thing was, I didn't have my license yet so I shouldn't have been working in a shop. There are people who belittle the barber trade because barbers often make their own schedules, and we are in a very relaxed environment. They think that my job consists of making my own schedule and goofing off in the shop all day and not really making much money.

History says that tonsure artist not only cut hair and performed shaves, but they were also dentists and executed bloodletting. Most people think that the barber pole means barbershop, and they are sadly mistaken. The barber pole explains a lot about how important my craft is. The red stands for blood; the blue stands for veins; the white stands for bandages; and the silver ball at the bottom is where the blood would run. Our licenses came from the same place that doctors and nurses received theirs. We could also be responsible for the death of a human being. For example, there is a lot that barbers and cosmetologist have to learn, but there are some things that are really important, such as bacteriology, anatomy, physiology, and sanitation—just to name a few. It was in the late 1800s when the professions were separated into individual professions. Cosmetologists as well as barbers can be responsible for someone's death. That's why it is important to have the proper training, take the state board exam and obtain a license to deem you qualified to be a professional barber stylist.

I saved my money. In turn, my dad found a location in Matteson for me to rent so that I could become the first black barbershop in Matteson. I made history, and again most people thought this barbershop was just put in my hands, not knowing that no one had given me any money to open it. I had to save my money, fix up and open my own barbershop.

Along with my father, uncles, and cousins, we put down carpet, tile, built stations, put up mirrors and lights, and a friend of mine painted. I started with three barber chairs and worked my way up. I worked hard to put my barbershop together, and yet, I still had something missing. I continued to get kicked out of barber school, which meant that while I owned and operated my own business, I did not have the credentials. I had to go back and finish school, but even though I finished school, I never obtained enough theory in order to pass my state board exam, so I ended up taking the test two times and failed twice. What was I going to do? Cutting hair in a salon without a license could land you in jail if you run into the wrong judge, because it's illegal. It can cause your business to be shut down, along with me being disciplined and not being able to get my license. I opened up my shop at nineteen, so I really didn't have time to concentrate on getting my license. I wasn't worried. There are a million shops, so who would come to my shop and bother me about not having a license? I didn't believe anything like that could ever happen.

Time passed and Larry's Barber Shop was the hot spot in Matteson for a good hair cut. It didn't matter what race, color or creed you were. If you had hair, we could cut it. Business got so good, I had to start opening up the barbershop at 4:30 a.m. to accommodate different customers' schedules.

"Where do I go from here?" I thought. I made so much money as a young man. It reached a point that I looked like I had a lot of money. I started frivolously spending. I bought a new pair of rims for my car whenever I felt like it. I purchased radios and speakers and the low rider kit with a Batman wing on the top. I bought every piece of jewelry you could think of. I always had my clothes tailored and purchased alligator shoes in every color.

"Nothing could stop me now," I thought. Not to mention, I was already popular because of who my dad being was in the music industry and due to his being a business owner. Everybody knew "Lil Larry." And the women were lined up. I use to sleep with two to three women every day almost. My behavior was disgraceful. I liked older women, especially since they had their own place, and they were more mature. They helped me to grow up fast sexually and assisted me with life's struggles. They would give me money along with letting me drive their cars, and they would buy me nice gifts. All I had to do was put it down good and make them feel like a real woman and listen to them. I was always in hotels. I sometimes slept with two or three women at one time. I was living the life. I thought nothing could stop me. My stamina and endurance increased because each woman was different, so each encounter brought forth a different high. I didn't care what color the woman was. I think I covered almost every race of women that existed, and I was out of control. I was a smooth talker and could convince women to sleep with me within the first couple hours of meeting them. I would even have sex with girls in the barber shop or next door in the beauty shop. I was only being a man, I thought. To prevent from spending money for a hotel, I even stooped as low as to have sex with women outside in the parks or on the side of the expressways. The key thing for me was not telling my friends. I didn't want to mess up what I had from them hating.

The girls would always tell their girlfriends. Then their girlfriends would end up wanting to sleep with me. I didn't care. It was more for me. I had all of this going for me: a great business, money, clothes, and women. But then the reality set in. My barbershop was running off commission, which meant that I had to pay all of the barbers with a check. The only problem with that was the barbers were putting in more tickets than they cut, which meant I came up short all the time, and there would never be enough money to meet payroll.

"What was I missing?" I thought. Even though I was a hard worker, I didn't have a clue how to professionally run the day-to-day business, as far as the finances were concerned. I was pretty smart and computer literate, but no one told me these business skills were necessary. I just thought I was suppose to make money and enjoy everything that came along with it.

CHAPTER **4**

Mismanaging
THE BARBERSHOP

MISMANAGING THE BARBERSHOP

There was no big overhead in operating a barbershop, so how could my business start going down? Along with not having my license, I had no business plan and no financial stability in running my barbershop. The banks refused to give me any loans, except one I obtained for $3,000, which was very little money. Still, I was immature. I figured I had room for improvement, but the stress of everything caused me to be angry often (I thought). I would have fistfights with my barbers. I threw clippers at clients who made me upset. I had begun to really start falling apart and didn't have a clue as to why. I wanted to blame everyone else. What was I suppose to do?

Before you knew it, all of the rent and utility bills started falling behind. The building manager would come in the barbershop in front of everyone and give me a five-day notice and made me sign it. How embarrassing that was for everyone to see me get a notice that stated if I didn't pay my rent plus late charges by a certain time, the doors of my barbershop would get locked. On top of that, the phone, gas, electric, and water bill were due. The bill collectors would call while I was standing up cutting hair, and I would have to whisper and make payment arrangements because I was too embarrassed to let anyone hear me. I'm asked myself, "Why was all of this happening to me?" I am in church and living the way I was taught to live so I shouldn't have any problems. Little did I know, it starts first natural and then spiritual, which meant that I wasn't exempt from problems, but I wasn't trying to hear that! I had been living my life exceptionally well, so I felt as though I deserved every good I had coming.

My Blazer was one of the hottest SUVs on the streets, but I didn't expect to get pulled over every single day because the police thought I was a drug dealer. How dare the police pull me over? I am a legit business man, so I told them that they needed to pull over and scope out the people who were the real gangbangers and drug dealers. Then I realized how my car looked, so I brought that on myself. I wasn't a drug dealer, so if they wanted to search my car, I let them search it. Then I would get back in my car and go. As time progressed, nothing was going right for me. I started playing drums for different community choirs and also anyone else who asked me to play. I wasn't twenty-one yet, so there were certain things I had to talk over with my parents before I did them. For instance, I had a secular gig at a cultural center, and it so happen to be on a Friday night, which was the same night as church service. I asked my dad if I could go, and he told me to ask my my grandmother.

I did ask her, and she said OK, as long as I came to church first. I was excited because I didn't think she was going to let me go. We practiced for weeks for this gig, and I had to use my drums, so I took them and sat them up earlier that day. I got to the gig that night, and it was an adult atmosphere, which meant they were drinking and smoking. I'm not bothered by it since I don't do either, so it didn't affect me. There was thirty minutes left before it was time to go on, and through the crowd, I see my father walk up. He came up to me and said, "Get your drums and let's go!"

I'm thinking, "What's going on? you said I could play!"

He repeated, "Get your drums and let's go!" I did believe it. I told him I can't take my drums because they don't have another drum set. My cousin ended up playing the drums instead of the piano. The band director understood, so he allowed me to still pick up part of my check. I went over to his home on that following day to get my check. I got out of my car in front of his apartment complex, and a man jumped in my car with a key, started it up and pulled off. I called my dad and said, "Someone just jumped in my car with a key and stole it!"

He had to come pick me up. I later found out that my SUV had been repossessed. Oh my God!! What was happening? I later discovered that the finance company received my check, but it was misplaced. It was as if I hadn't made my payment. My dad made arrangements, and I was able to go and get my truck back.

I'm thinking I'm the big baller and shot caller, so I go and pick my sister up from school one day. I decide I want to go and buy another car. I went up to the Ford dealership, and I bought a used pearl-white Mustang with a burgundy drop top and five-star rims. My credit was A1. I had twenty-two credit cards—all in good standing—and now, in addition to a Blazer, I owned a convertible Mustang. These were two of the most popular cars on the streets at the time. My sister told me, "Daddy is gonna get you!"

I replied, "I'm grown, and I work hard and have to pay the note, so he can't make that decision for me." My sister drove my truck home, and I drove the Mustang with the top down in 50-degree weather. My mom called me on my cellular phone after my sister got home and she asked me, "Where are you?"

I said, "In the car!"

She said, "What car?"

I replied, "My new car!"

She said, "Your daddy is gonna get you!" And she hung up the phone. What did I have to worry about? The car was in my name, so can't nobody tell me nothing. It was cold outside, but I still drove around my friends' neighborhoods so they could see my new car. It was a Monday night, so I had to go to church. I couldn't wait for everyone to see my new car. I got home and my dad said, "Take it back!"

I said, "No, I'm not.

My dad said, "Either take it back or you gotta get out of this house." Being true to my zodiac sign—I'm a Taurus—I was very stubborn. I said, "OK, I'm leaving."

I started packing my things. He said, "Leave the keys to the Blazer on the table."

"That's my car," I said. "I pay the car note, so I will be back to get my other car."

It was one big mess. My mother came to my room and said, "Larry, please take the car back will you."

So I used that for an excuse as to why I took the car back: because my mother asked me to. I took the car back and my father walked in with me, and the salesman knew dad from the restaurant.

My dad sat the keys on the desk and said we were bringing the car back; however, the man told him he couldn't do that. My dad said I have been buying cars for over twenty years. I have thirty days to return this car. I was boiling at this point, and I told my dad that's OK. I was still going to buy a Lexus. My dad said "Yeah, when you get your own garage to park it in!" I told my father he was just jealous of me because I was able to have two nice cars at a young age. My parents were appalled. My mother said, "Don't you ever say that to your father ever again."

I was young and immature and the wrong things were important to me, so I apologized. The paperwork with the finance charges came about two weeks later and my father opened it and said, "Do you realize they were going to charge you 28 percent?" He told me that I would be paying for that car almost twice. In the end, my dad was right, and I was wrong.

I only had liability insurance on my Blazer, so I wasn't fully protected if I had an accident. Sure enough, I had my first accident, which wasn't my fault, and the police verified that. The officer didn't give me or the lady who hit me a ticket. We exchanged information and she said her insurance would take care of the damages. Well, that never happened, and I was not covered and neither did I have the $5,000 to get my Blazer fixed, so it sat in the dealership's parking lot. So, now I'm without any transportation. Winter was coming and my sister was to graduate from high school soon. At 17, she decided she wanted to go to beauty school, so she paid her way through beauty school. She got married and had a baby, but the marriage didn't last. So she moved back into our parents' home. She was driving one of my mom's cars, and the heat went out. I went out and bought her another car because I didn't want her driving to school with my nephew in a car with no heat in the winter. You couldn't have paid anyone not to think we were rich, and boy, was that a great feeling!

CHAPTER 5

BECOMING AN ADULT

SUICIDE IS NOT THE ANSWER

I turned twenty-one, and I just knew I was grown and I could do whatever I wanted to do. I was standing in my barbershop cutting hair one day, and I picked up the phone and called my mother. It had just hit me that I was molested when I was a child, so I had to tell someone. I was between the ages of two and five years old, so I really had no clue what was going on back then or how it would manifest as I got older. My mom said, "Well son, they already got enough on them. You are a strong man, and it didn't affect you, so don't worry about it."

"Yes, I know," I told her. "I just had to share it with someone." Being molested caused me to be perverted at a young age, always trying to play house with every girl that I was around, it really didn't matter who. There were still rules and regulations that I had to abide by. My mother was old-fashioned, which meant that until I moved out and paid my own mortgage, I still had to abide by my parents' rules. I met a young lady at the pancake house. She was the woman of my dreams, I thought. I insisted that she become my girlfriend. It was settled: she liked me, and I liked her. In the first few weeks, I told her mom that she was going to be my wife, and her mom looked at me like I was crazy and said, "Yeah, OK. That's nice."

This girl was in college, and she was intelligent. She could do whatever she wanted to do pretty much, so I felt as though I needed to have the same profile. My father still insisted that I be in at a decent hour. I begged and pleaded with my parents. I didn't drink, smoke, use drugs or party. I would just be out with my girlfriend. It didn't matter to them. I still had to be home at a certain time of the night, so I just tried to abide by those rules.

Time went on, and I still was without my car, and she would come and pick me up and drop me off. Sometimes, she would even let me keep her car. What a perfect situation, I thought, even though her car was a stick shift and I always stalled at the light. Eventually, I got it right. We dated for a period of time, so I took her to church with me to show her off to my family and friends, but there was still a problem. She was the opposite of the young lady whom I was suppose to marry because she wore pants, makeup and went to clubs. That wasn't acceptable, so I tried to convince her that none of this was right, and we couldn't walk together unless we were equally yoked. She disagreed, but we remained a couple, and everything was going great.

I was standing in my barbershop cutting my father's hair, and my girlfriend, at the time, called me and said, "I am pregnant."

I'm thinking how could that be if you are taking birth control pills? I hung up the phone, and at this time, I'm trying to figure out what am I going to do. I am a church boy, and we are not suppose to have sex until we get married, let alone have a baby. I said to my father, "Guess what?"

He said, "What?"

I said my girl friend is pregnant and he said, "Well, there goes your Lexus!" My dad was very understanding, and I appreciated the fact that he allowed me to mature and not fuss at me.

My best friend and I were at the park one day playing basketball, and he was talking about moving to Indiana and he needed a roommate. I told him I would move in. That was the perfect opportunity for me to move out of my parents' house so I could do what I wanted to do. I just wanted to feel like I was grown. We moved in together, and he was rarely there because he was always at his mom's house or over his girlfriend's house, so I had it made. I had just bought a Mercedes-Benz, so I had transportation again. I was living the dream. I still had good credit, but I didn't understand the legal aspect of handling certain business and buying a car was one of them.

The dealership sent me through a secondary finance company, so they could make more money. I end up paying a 22 percent finance charge, but I didn't have a clue. I was paying an $800 monthly car note, and I could handle it because I made a lot of money, so I didn't care. Business was good, but I still hadn't got a handle on the business end of having a barbershop. So, things started getting out of control. About six or seven months went by, and I started falling behind on my car note, so I was on the repossession list for three or four months. The good part was the repo company didn't have my Indiana address, which bought me an extra few days to pay my car note. This company didn't give you 30 to 45 days; I was put on the repossession list the day after my due date.

It was winter, and the heater inside my barbershop went out. I got it fixed, but the repair man told me that the furnace on the roof was old, and it wasn't going to last long. I called the management company, and they said that it wasn't their problem, and I had to fix on my own. I didn't have any extra money to get a new furnace. Needless to say, the furnace went out again, and there was no fixing it. To top it off, the snow on the roof was leaking down through a broken drain into the barbershop.

I couldn't believe all of this was happening. My father had his restaurant, but he also had responsibilities and obligations because his overhead was over the top. It was embarrassing that the barbers in my shop were cutting hair in hats, gloves and a scarves. I had to buy some mini heaters, but they only worked a little. To add to the freezing cold, most of the ceiling tiles started to leak. They got soaked to the degree that they fell down onto the floor—only slightly missing the customers. I had to stand up there and cut hair despite getting talked about, as well as feeling humiliated. My barbers understood and they stuck by my side until things got better. I eventually stopped commission with my barbers and went to booth rental. This worked out better because I could budget better on a weekly basis. I had a set amount of money I could depend on every week. On top of all of this, I still didn't have my barber's license, so one day an inspector came in the barber shop and said, "Hello, may I please speak with the owner?"

I said, "Yes, that's me."

And he said, "I need to see everyone's licenses, please."

No one in the shop had a license. What am I to do I thought? He said we had to close and couldn't operate until we obtained our licenses. I can't close my business down, I thought. I told the man I would, but I reopened anyway and took a chance. My chance lasted for awhile. Christmas time came around, and I figured I would ask my girlfriend to marry me. I sent my mom to the mall with my credit card and had her to buy an engagement ring for me, and she did just that. I proposed at Christmas, and it was settled that we were getting married.

Time went on, and I felt as if my prayers had been answered by God because things started getting better. They came and installed a new furnace and finally fixed the drain that was leaking inside the barbershop. Spring passed and summer came. I decided I was going to move back home with my parents, so while they were at the restaurant, I paid one of my barbers $100 to help me move from Indiana back to Matteson. I went back to the barbershop, and when my parents got home, all of my furniture and everything was in their den. They told me that I had a lot of nerve.

"Hey, I'm your child," I said. "And I have every right to move back home. I didn't ask to be back here."

I'm lucky I didn't get slapped in my mouth. At any rate, I appreciated their accepting me back home.

My daughter, Emani, was born August 27, 1994, and I was the happiest person in the world. I took my baby to church to let my grandmother see her, and she said she didn't want to see no baby who was born out of wedlock. I was very hurt. My grandmother's attitude made my daughter's mom feel as if we might not be good for one another. Of course, that made me start getting upset with everyone. I felt as though they were making my fiancée change her mind about me. Still, we continued to work on our relationship.

We decided to go to the zoo with my daughter, and we talked about everything, and I told her that we would be OK. I was very insecure about who she hung out with, so maybe should monitor that. I really didn't want anyone getting into her head and swaying her from church. We were driving home from the zoo, and I thought everything was fine, but it wasn't. She was the type of person who really didn't like to share her feelings, but she would say things that made me feel as if I wasn't good enough for her. I ended up punching her windshield and breaking it. Boy did I have a temper, but I never paid it any mind because I felt as though everyone gets upset. Then when I thought about it, I made her feel like she wasn't good enough for me because I tried to conform her into someone who I wanted her to be, and that wasn't fair to her. I began understanding where her frustration may have come from.

What was wrong with me? I never thought it was me. I always thought it was everyone else, which made me not to ever seek counseling. I couldn't think of anything I could have gone through or anything that I was going through, so I figured I was fine. Needless to say, time progressed and my woman decided that it wasn't best that we remain together as a couple. I was devastated. This was my first love ever and on top of that we had a daughter together. I couldn't believe it. I tried to reason with her, but it was no use. It was over.

Here I go again; I started back on the women tip. I could convince a woman to sleep with me the first day I met her. I thought I had game. This was normal because women only wanted what you wanted, but most men thought they had to lie to get with them. I was always honest. If they weren't my girlfriends we didn't go for dinner, to the show or anything else couples did. We just had good sex. I was very picky, so I had to be with a good clean woman, and I made sure I used protection because I didn't want no diseases, nor did I want any more kids. They said that the preacher kids were always the worse and I wondered why that was. It was because we were bound as children and young adults. We figured when we got older that we were going to let it all out. I had great parents, and I tried to follow in their footsteps and do everything as they would do. I appreciated them for being good examples. Of course, they wanted me to wait until I got married to have sex and have children, but that was a little out of my control. I wanted to sleep with women. I didn't want to smoke, curse, drink, sell drugs, gangbang or use drugs. What sense would that have made? To a certain degree, I was very judgmental of people who did all of these things. I couldn't figure out for the life of me what sense it made to do things that could cause your life to go down the drain, especially if it was abused. One thing I didn't realize was that being a womanizer was just as bad as all of those things I named, but I didn't know that I had that problem because being with a woman was natural, so I was fine as far as I was concerned.

I decided that I wanted to open up a barbershop in the city. I was tired of the suburbs. This was right after my dad convinced me to trade my Mercedes in and get an Eddie Bauer Ford Explorer. My dad couldn't pay me to put food and sauce in my car because I was afraid it would spill, but when it meant opening my own business, I did what I had to do. I had moved equipment in my Mercedes, so I had messed up the leather seats. All in all, I never wanted it to appear that I wasn't making my own decisions, so of course, that had to be my reason for trading the Mercedes in. He told me that my rates would be much better, and it would give me an opportunity to breathe, so I did it. Later, I met a guy who was a barber and he was interested in buying into my business. I thought about it, and it was the perfect way out of the suburbs, but we were partners.

His goals were different from mine, which caused us to have some conflicts. I am a leader, but I can follow as well when it is necessary, so that's how I was able to hold on. I started working on the barbershop in Chicago located at 103rd and Halsted Streets. My best friend and I were very close, so I decided that I wanted him to be a part of my barbershop. He didn't know anything about the business, but because he trusted me, there was no doubt whether the

business would be run correctly. This is my livelihood, so I had no other choice but to do what I knew to do. I am a very honest person, so there was nothing for him to worry about. We had another guy who was involved, but he decided to drop out at the last minute. We went on to fix the place up without any assistance from the banks, which meant we had to finance it on our own. We had to wing it each day and make the best out of the situation, but we were determined to succeed. The shop was located in a new strip mall, so there were no stores open yet. I had applied for my license and passed all my inspections, so I was actually able to open before anyone else. Also, the pavement wasn't finished yet, but it was OK. Clients didn't mind. I had opened my second barbershop, and boy was I happy!

Since I'd opened my new shop, I decided to legally cut all ties with my partner in Matteson, so I sold him the barbershop as a whole. He agreed, and so I was all good. It was on. I thought about how I could help people and sow into their lives because I had seen the way my mom and dad always looked out for people. My dad would give people free food from his restaurant when they couldn't feed their families, and he would create jobs for them, so they could work. If my mom found out that anybody inside or outside of church didn't have groceries or furniture, she would get a crew together and go to that family's aid. They did this purely as a gesture from their hearts.

I strived very hard to pattern myself after my parents because I looked up to them. I decided I wanted to feed the homeless, so I found a way to reach out to whomever I could. I wanted this to be steady, so I went underneath lower Wacker Drive in Chicago's downtown area and found about thirty people who lived down there. Every week, I wanted to make sure they had food to eat. I put myself in their shoes. I wouldn't want anybody to give me mess, so I didn't want to give them mess. I had my father to get me some big, hard plastic containers with lids for each individual down there. Every Monday, my day off, I went to the grocery store to shop for them. I didn't just take a bag of food down there and let them dig in; I individualized portions for each individual to last the person from Monday through Sunday. I packed them each different kinds of meats to choose from during the week: sodas, juices, toiletries, breads, water, toothbrushes, napkins, condiments, and anything else that would make them happy in their temporary state. When my mother and the group at the church had buffets, I would buy each individual a plate and fill it up with hot food that consisted of about fifteen different items, including all kinds of deserts. My daughter was only about six years old, and I took her with me to hand out food, and she asked me if she could help. Many homeless people recognized me from my barbershop and from being a musician. I was honored that I could not only help people, but I could help someone who knew me and didn't just see me as being a successful businessman. I was standing up in the barbershop cutting hair one day, and one of the homeless guys stuck his head in and said, "Larry, I would just like to say thanks, man. I made it from down there, and I found a job and a place to live." That meant more to me than you could imagine because I was able to assist that man and help him get another chance at life. I literally cried because it could have been me who was being fed. Sometimes, I would have only enough money to feed the homeless people, and I wouldn't have money left over for myself, but I didn't care. It was more important to me that they could depend on me every week like clockwork. I didn't do this to get glory from anyone, so I never told anyone. I just did it for over a year until they closed down lower Wacker Drive for construction. It could only get better, I thought.

CHAPTER 6

STABILITY

STABILITY

The word on the street is that being married shows stability, and that's what I wanted. Plus, we were taught in church that it was better to marry than to burn. My mom and dad were happily married, and that's what I've always wanted. So, I tried again to look for a wife. I was tired of sleeping around with any woman I could persuade to get into bed with me, so I looked for a stable situation. I figured that I would find me a church girl who I would be compatible with, so I started the search. We were often coaxed into dating women in my church, but I didn't feel as though there was anyone there good enough for me. So, I searched outside the church.

My grandmother went to Africa with some of her pastor friends from other cities. In preparation for a trip to Africa, there are certain measures you must take to stay healthy. My grandmother had a lot of faith and really didn't believe in taking medicine. Needless to say, she didn't take the necessary precautions for staying healthy.

In 1995, my grandmother started getting sick, and my gut feeling told me that she was getting ready to die. I called and checked on her one Monday morning, and she said, "I'm doing OK, grandson." But I wasn't satisfied with her response. We had church service that night, and she completely diverted from the normal service. She told everyone to line up in the middle aisle. She started hugging everyone in church and saying she loved us and for us to be good. At that moment, I knew she was getting ready to leave us. That Friday, she didn't come to church. She was hospitalized, but no one knew it. She didn't even want my mother to know because my mother couldn't have accepted that my grandmother had already made her mind up that it was her time to go on to be with the Lord. On that Friday night after service, we got a call that my grandmother had passed away. My mother became hysterical. She repeatedly screamed, "why didn't they tell me? They should have told me."

I believe that my grandmother wanted people to remember her as she was. She had never been seriously ill before. She didn't believe in going to doctors. It would have been unusual for someone to see her in that state. My grandmother sent word to me from her death bed that she loved me, and no matter what I did, I should stay saved and be successful. I promised, not only for myself, but for her I would do just that.

I started losing my zeal for being at my grandmother church since she was no longer living, so I decided to go and visit other churches. I had more free time on my hands musically, so I started playing for a community choir. This was a dream come true for me. I had the opportunity to write and record songs, and get paid writers' royalties. Things really turned around in my favor. I traveled all over the world, including Germany, London, Italy, and British Columbia—not to mention almost every state in the United States. I had songs that even made compilation albums. My father was a great organist and songwriter, so I was put in the same category as my dad. Playing for a community choir meant that people singing and playing were from all walks of life. I appreciated the experience that I got from being able to play in big arenas. The problem I had with being with multiple women intensified.

I met many stars and played on the same stages with many great performers such as MC Hammer, Kirk Franklin, Patti LaBelle, Albertina Walker, Percy Bady, Ricky Dillard— to name a few. I was treated like a star because I was a member of popular groups. Being able to have these musical experiences helped me to decide what kind of ministry I wanted to pursue. I started going to St. James C.O.G.I.C Church where Pastor Willie James Campbell was the pastor. This church was awesome. I ended up being a full-time drummer, and I also played the organ when needed.

Traveling and performing all over the world drew even more women to me. The womanizing just kept growing. If you were a musician, women didn't care if you were ugly, fat or stinky. As long as you were popular, the women loved you. Also having musical roots in church allowed me to get a good look at the women in the congregation, especially when they walked around during offering time. I would feel so ashamed at times because I would look out into the audience in church and see so many women that I had slept with. At times, some of them were sitting very close to each other. This wasn't right, and it wasn't me. It was a spirit that had a hold of me. I felt I needed to find me a wife and soon. I knew finding a wife wouldn't solve the problem of womanizing. I needed to be totally delivered from being a whore, but again I didn't realize I even had a problem.

I finally met a young lady I considered to be a wonderful woman. I became very fond of her and fell in love with her. She just happened to be the pastor's daughter. There couldn't have been a better woman for me. Like me, she was in church, and we had a lot in common. Fortunately, my family already knew her family from church ventures. Because my dad was in the music industry, we traveled in the same social circles. We dated and it was inevitable that we would get married. Therefore, we didn't waste any time. I got her a ring, and I proposed to her at the Chicago Bulls stadium on the large screen, as we sat courtside.

"Yes," she said. "I will marry you, Larry!"

I think I was overly excited because I did it in front of tens of thousands of Bulls fans.

I thought that I was the stuff.

Both of our parents suggested that we go to marriage counseling, but we figured, who needs marriage counseling? We were happy, we knew what we wanted, so there were no questions about us getting married. It was a done deal. We had a huge, extravagant wedding, and I was the happiest man alive. My daughter was able to be in the wedding without her mom being upset. I think it's only fair that if people move on, they shouldn't be spiteful. The children don't have anything to do with their past relationship. They are innocent, so you shouldn't put them in your mess.

My dream had finally come true. I fell in love and got married in October 1998. We found a beautiful apartment, which made things even better because we were both used to living a certain way. We went on a cruise for our honeymoon, and when we got back, life began.

We both had plenty, which meant we had a chance to really grow together financially and spiritually. I had always been into clothes and shoes. I wore suits and ties as well as casual clothes to school most of my life. I had collected a lot of valuable things, such as high-end clothes, shoes, musical instruments and equipment, and barber equipment. I was one who really believed in investing in the things I needed, especially my musical equipment. Consequently, I took care of everything I had. My wife was a hairdresser so I decided that we should open up another shop, but we would make it a full-service salon.

The marriage seemed to have been working out perfectly because we had so much in common. We had both been in church all of our lives, our parents were preachers, we were both in the hair business, she was a professional singer and I was a musician. What a dream come true! I was ready to live my life and be happy, but I didn't know about all the other stuff that came along with living with another individual. I wasn't prepared for that part of it. I thought when two people were happy, they lived in peace and harmony. In retrospect, we should have gone to marriage counseling. Since we didn't, we figured we would get through whatever obstacles there were.

I decided to open a tailor shop, since I was really into clothes. I took on a partner because I didn't know how to make clothes that well. In addition, I also started a limousine business simultaneously, which my grandfather had specialized in for more than twenty-five years, so I was just adding to the business. Wouldn't you know, I opened up right next door to my barbershop on 103rd and Halsted Street. My wife had her shop, and I had mine.

My wife started going out and singing on the road a lot, but it was OK because I was in the same field, and I understood. Actually, we sometimes had to sing or play for the same people.

Competition started sneaking into our marriage. Also, we really didn't understand our roles as husband and wife. There were times I may have been short paying the bills at home, and she felt as if I wasn't a man if I had to ask for her help. Wow, I thought! I thought we were supposed to work together on everything, but I thought wrong in this case. What made matters even worse is that when we had problems, we talked to other people when we should have talked to each other or gone to a counselor. She would want to continue the arguments and called my barbershop to talk about things while I was there working. I would get very upset, and it would ruin my day, which caused me to start acting out again. I slammed the phone down and broke it. I got in the car and punched my rear view mirror and broke it. She made me so angry that I smashed a couple of cell phones. I had a serious problem! I had to get a grip on things, but I didn't know how.

One day, she called the barbershop and wanted to argue. I wasn't going for it; so, I didn't get on the phone. She told one of my barbers to inform me that my things would be in the front of our apartment building. Of course, I had to rush out and go home. Fortunately my things weren't outside. They were pushed by the door. In other words, she was trying to tell me to get my things and go. I took her up on it. I got my things, loaded up my Navigator and went back to work. I had a lot of stuff, so it was only enough room for me to drive. I went and found an apartment that same day in Lake Meadows on King Drive in Chicago. I couldn't move in for a few weeks. My best friend was living in Prairie Shores, which was about two blocks from Lake Meadows. I stayed with him until my place was ready. My wife and I were separated. Everyone who knew me pretty much figured it wasn't because of anything in particular that I did. The split was due to both of us being immature and not knowing how to handle a marriage.

Since I played an active role at her dad's church, she wanted to make sure that her family to side with her. However, her dad felt as though our problems had nothing to do with him; therefore, my position in his church wasn't threatened. I was his right-hand man. It wasn't about a paycheck. It was about me loving him and the ministry and doing whatever I could to help the ministry move to the next level. That's what I did. I was just like my dad. I paid musicians out of my own pocket for their participation in the ministry, and I filled in any gaps I could without complaining. My father-in-law gave me keys to the church. He would also allow me to purchase things for the church, and he would sign checks and let me fill them out for whatever I needed to get for the church. That was trust; therefore, I never abused that privilege. My wife and I decided to get back together. We were in love, so we tried it again. She had already moved back home with her parents, so it was an easy transition because she just moved right in with me at my place in Lake Meadows.

CHAPTER 7

WAKE-UP CALL

Our apartment in Lake Meadows was only a one bedroom. It was very small, but we made the best of it. We had to use the living room for closet space as well as the hall closet. We sat and talked about things that transpired while we were separated, but it didn't matter to me. The only things I was concerned about was our being happy and together. I had learned my lesson before about asking questions about things that I really couldn't handle hearing about. Knowing things that your woman may have been involved in her past could really mess you up mentally, and I didn't want to go through that anymore because I would find myself competing with a man I didn't even know. I guess this was in order to prove to my wife that I was better and more mature. She told me that she wanted to pursue her music career full time, and I didn't have any say so on the matter. I agreed mainly to keep peace.

One day, we got into a heated argument. I was good for yelling, but this time, it became so bad that it escalated into a physical altercation. I would never hit a woman, but I had to keep her off of me because she was very emotional, which I understood; however, I wasn't going to let her hit or kick me. I tried to leave the apartment, but she wouldn't let me. I finally pulled away, and I ran downstairs. I called my best friend and he came and met me outside. He asked me what was I doing. I said she called the police, and I'm waiting on them to get here. He told me that if she called the police, they would take me.

I said, I didn't do anything. He said that didn't matter. She called the police, therefore, they would take me into custody. So, I left and went down to her dad's church and told him what happened. I called down to the police station to see if I needed to come in or anything, and they said that there was no record, so no charges had been filed. I stayed away from the apartment until later that night. When I entered my apartment, I got a surprise. She had her mom, brother and his friends come and move all of her things out. She was done. That's not all; not only did they move her things out, but they also took all of my stuff. There were 150 bottles of cologne missing, 300 neckties, 35 to 40 tailor-made suits, 50 to 60 pairs of shoes, a bass guitar and amplifier, 10 pairs of prescription glasses, 10 designer sweaters, diamond rings, nugget rings, bracelets and pretty much anything else they could take. On top of that, they took my toothbrushes, put them in the toilet and urinated on them. They took my shower gels and poured them in the bathtub and ran water in it. They took all of my business checkbooks and wrote all over the checks, making comments about me. The rest of my dresser drawers were ransacked. I was left with only the items I had at the cleaners, the shoes I had on, and three other pairs of shoes.

I called and told my parents, and I went and told her father. He got on the phone and said I'm going to get all of your stuff back right now. I told him no. Let them keep it all. I didn't want it back—it wouldn't be the same.

I had decided that there was no use in living because I didn't want to get divorced. We were taught in church that you are not supposed to. I tried to cut my throat with my car keys, but I didn't try hard enough because it didn't work. I just decided that I would straighten up and try to get my life back on track. I had the lady who cleaned my barbershop everyday to come and get my apartment back in order. I was fine. There were a lot of ways I could have dealt with the situation, but I chose to deal with it on a positive note. All of my friends wanted to intervene, but I said no. I wasn't going for it. I would be fine. I was going to let God deal with it.

The incident happened on a Monday. On Wednesday I went to work. Later, I left to pick my daughter up from school. I took her to her house and helped her with her homework. I went back to the barbershop, and I sat down to play chess with the other barbers. Not long after that, some police officers came in and asked for Larry Roberts, and I said "that's me." They asked if they could talk to me privately, so we went back by the restroom. They told me that they had gotten a complaint, and they needed to take me in to sign a document, but I would be right back out. I gave my car keys to my best friend and told him to call my parents, and tell them that I was going to the police station, just in case anything happened. They told me they had to put me in handcuffs. I said I had never been in any trouble, let alone get put in handcuffs. The police said it was a requirement.

They took me to the police station on 111th Street. When we got there, they took the cuffs off, and one of the officers told me, "We had to tell you that so you wouldn't get feisty, but they are going to keep you."

I was outdone. I was in a cold cell without a coat, and when my parents arrived, the police told them that I wasn't there. I was locked up with people who had domestic cases ranging from cutting their spouse to beating up family members. I was thinking, "I don't belong here. I didn't do nothing."

I went for fingerprinting, and I asked the officer what was the procedure. He told me I would go to domestic court, but I would be home by lunch the next day. He also said, "O.J. has messed it up for everyone!"

Needless to say, I couldn't really sleep. I was in a place I never dreamed I would ever be.

It was about 5 a.m. the next morning, and they prepared us to go to court, or so I thought. We were handcuffed in pairs. They put us on a truck that looked like a wholesale truck, and at this point, I'm really in shock. The guys started talking about going to the Cook County Jail, and I told them that the police officer that did the fingerprinting said we were going to court then home, but they said we going to the County. I said, "We will see."

We went to other police stations and picked up more

prisoners, and the truck started getting packed. We were squeezed in like sardines, until there was standing room only. There were guys on the truck bragging about who they killed and why they deserved it. At this point, I'm saying to myself, "I don't belong on here."

I wasn't afraid because I considered myself a man and would fight if I had to. The point was, I didn't do anything to deserve being in this position. We were on the truck passing all the familiar streets, and I was looking for us to pull up at 13th Street and Michigan Avenue for domestic court; however, the truck started backing up in the gate of 26th Street and California Avenue. I couldn't believe this. They made us get off and removed the cuffs, and we lined up in the back to be processed. When the other group got done with the first step of processing, they brought us in. We were told that now was the time to put anything that we shouldn't have in the middle of the floor. Some did just that. Others didn't bother. We then went into the next room and they called us up and wrote numbers all over our hands and arms with black markers. The cells were filled to capacity. People were standing, sitting or lying on the floor. I wasn't sitting on a dirty floor, so I found a good seat. This started at 7 a.m. We went from bullpen (as they refer to it) to bullpen in order to be processed. At this point, I was in there with people whom had done anything and everything because we hadn't made it to the point where we were separated into categories according to what we were charged with doing and how many times we had been to jail.

I was sitting in the bullpen in the afternoon when they

called 382, which was my number. I wondered who could be
calling. I was pretty well-known, so word had gotten around
that I was in the County. It was my attorney and my dad.
Then, my best friend got on the phone and asked me if I was
OK, and I said I would be cool. I went back to my bullpen.
All of us had to go back out to go to court. I was thinking
that we were going out but court was merely looking into
a camera that was set up in the basement of the jail with a
judge that stated our bond amounts. My bond was $5,000.
Compared to everyone else who had domestic charges of
$200 or $300 dollars, mine seemed excessive. When I was
done, they called my number again and handed me a phone.
It was my attorney and my dad. I told them I hadn't done
anything so don't bond me out because I didn't want them to
lose their money. I said I would beat it. When I was finishing
up on the phone with them another phone rang. An officer
asked if there was a Larry Roberts down here, and I said yes.
I got the phone and it was a correctional officer who knew
me. There was nothing no one could do, so I had to continue
going through the process. We went to the next phase. We had
to get shots, have our chests X-rayed, and they had to stick
a long metal Q-tip up our penises to check for any STDs. It
was torture. There were people in my cell who were "dope
sick," as it was called. This meant they needed a fix, and
because they didn't have one, they were on the floor sick.
The officers wouldn't do anything about it. I was so tired
of sitting down, I gave my seat up. I went from standing to
lying on the floor, the same dirty floor that I said I wouldn't
sit on. At this point, I didn't care. I was tired. I saw so many

people in there I knew. I was embarrassed to be there on top of everything else.

Every time I walked past an officer, they would stop me and say, "Don't I know you?" They would recall that I was Larry from the barber shop or Larry from church. I really couldn't believe this. We went down this long cold hallway to do a strip search, and it smelled very badly. The odor wasn't coming from me. I was very deep into personal hygiene. I still smelled like cologne, and I had enough deodorant on. We had to take off all of our clothes and put them on a yellow line that was about two feet in front of us. We had to face the wall and squat. How humiliating this was, but I didn't have a choice in the matter. After things checked out, they made us put our clothes back on; however, at their command, and piece by piece. By the time I got on my underwear, socks and pants, my uncle came down the hallway, and I called his name. He said "come on." Everyone was looking at me trying to figure out who I was and why I had a special privilege. I asked him if I could put the rest of my stuff on, and he said, "Man yeah. Go ahead"

He had me walked up to my cell privately by another officer. It was about 11 p.m., and I was beat. They had finally given us something to eat, which was some bread, lunch meat with green and red specs in it, an orange, and a juice that was sealed. I wasn't eating that mess. I gave it away for another juice, and I drank them both.

The only thing I dreaded about going to jail was having to say whether I was a part of a gang. I went up "on deck," as it was called. They opened the door and there were about five people standing there, and they each asked me, "What you ride?" This meant what gang was I in. I told them I don't ride nothing, and I stepped back and prepared for the worse, but nothing happened. They just told me to read the rules and the regulations, which I did. One rule stated that I had to take a shower, so I did. I had to get some shower shoes, and this guy called me over and said, "hey man, get those shower shoes instead." He said "those belong to the nation." I was like, whatever, but I did because it didn't matter to me one way or the other. There was blood all over the shower. I guess people had gotten jumped on, but again there was nothing I could do. I just had to weather the storm. The guy I got my bath towel from asked me for it back once I got through, and he put it on the radiator let it dry then folded it up and put it back up. I couldn't believe I had dried off with a towel that was not clean. This was the pits. I layed down and before you knew it they got us up about 5 a.m. to prepare for court.

We finally got to 13th Street and Michigan. I was glad because I was closer to going home. There were about ten guys in each bullpen waiting for court. They gave us food, and once again I traded it for a juice. Then this one guy turned around, pulled his pants down, sat on the toilet and used it in front of everyone. Then he just pulled his pants back up. Unbelievable, I thought. I needed to hurry up and get out of here. It was my turn to go in before the judge. I had on a Department Of Corrections uniform and shoes with no strings in them.

Inside the courtroom was my dad and my wife, who was

leaning on his shoulder crying. She didn't know that it would go to this degree. My case was dropped, and the state tried to pick it back up, but they didn't succeed. It was settled the next night. I was going home.

Being in jail taught me how to be patient. There was nothing that I could do but wait and be patient. We went back on the sheriff's bus, and boy was I excited. I started messing with the guys who were coming from court and had to go back to jail. When we got back to the County, we had to do another strip search. When we were putting our clothes back on, I was so excited. I wasn't thinking clearly, and I put all my clothes on at once, forgetting that I was supposed to put each piece of clothing on at the officer's command.

The officer said, "What the &%$# are you doing? Now, everyone take everything back off and start over, and thank this guy right here."

I was embarrassed. The guys were looking at me as if they were angry, but I didn't care because I wasn't a punk. So what? I was going home. A guy who worked in the lunchroom came up to me and said he got word to look out for me. I said, "cool." I didn't want any food. I went through the process in order to prepare to go home the next day. When my mom and dad picked me up, I was just happy to be getting out.

My attorney said he wanted to meet with my wife and me, and we did later on that night. I told her, let's scratch everything that happened and start all over. We tried, but needless to say, as time progressed it was obvious that our marriage was really over. I bought a three-flat building and a single-family home at the same time. The single-family home belonged to a woman name Minnie Straud. She was still living in the home, but I was unaware that I bought the house from a company that bought people's taxes. I was made out to be the villain because this elderly lady didn't know that she was $4,000 behind in her taxes. It made the front page of the newspaper. Everyone was looking at me saying I was a bad person. The radio stations were calling me and so was the mayor's office. Jesse Jackson went out to her house and was on television. There was a fund called the indemnity fund, which helped senior citizens to buy their properties back if they were in distress, and she needed to come up with $100,000. The fund was depleted. My wife found out about everything that was going on through the media, so she called me and demanded she get some of the money that I would be paid because she was my wife, and she felt she deserved it. She didn't understand that I had to give that money to the mortgage company to pay back the loan. I ended up just paying the mortgage on the home for about two months, and I reversed the deal so she could keep her house.

In November of 2000, my wife and I got divorced. I called my daughter's mom and told her that I was a free man, and if she wanted to give us another try, she should come on and do it now. Otherwise, I was moving on. I figured that she was my first love, and it would be OK. I really wanted to be married because I needed that stability in my life. So on December 2, 2000, we got married in my godmother's living room. Who cared if it wasn't a big ceremony? We could have a big wedding later. Boy, did we have a big wedding later on July 1, 2001. Between rings, clothes, food, and the mansion we had the wedding in, we were out about $30,000. But that's what she wanted, so I had no other choice. It was one of the most beautiful, extravagant events I had ever experienced. Outside, we had doves released. We also had a horse and carriage. You name it, we did it because we felt as though we deserved it.

CHAPTER 8

ANOTHER CHANCE

SUICIDE IS NOT THE ANSWER

I had a building that I sold, and after that, I moved into a house my new wife had bought. We fixed it up together. My building was on the west side of Chicago, and there were problems with it. I had tenants who were either always late with their rent, or I had to find them in order to collect payment. They were always in and out of jail, so I had to do a posting in order to put them out legally. Then during the winter months, they would get their gas turned off due to nonpayment, which caused the pipes to burst. I was sick of dealing with it. I was happy that I was able to sell.

I thought I was finally with the woman I've always wanted to be with, and our daughter, Emani, had both parents in the same home with her. We could raise her correctly. We didn't go to marriage counseling. We knew we belonged together, so who needed marriage counseling? I messed up shortly after we were married. We had a large communication gap that I tried over and over to resolve. I guess, at the time, it wasn't for me to understand. So I took matters into my own hands. There was a young lady I had gone to grammar and high school with. She was married and lived in another state. She and I would talk from time to time. Her husband knew about our conversations, but I hadn't told my wife that I talked to her. It was very innocent, and I enjoyed talking to her because it gave me hope in my marriage. One particular night, a friend of mine wanted to talk, so he came by my house and picked me up so I could go riding with him. After I got home, my wife told me she had been through my two-way pager and had seen the emails the girl and I had been sending to one another. It wasn't anything incriminating, but the fact was, I was talking to a young lady I shouldn't have been talking to because my wife didn't know about it. I told her I wouldn't talk to her anymore, but I did anyway.

As time went on, my wife had my cell phone bill transferred to her aunt's house, and she intercepted it in order to check my call activity. She came in the house while I was asleep and pointed out that I had been talking to this other woman at all times of the day and night. I immediately got upset. I jumped up and punched four holes in the walls. There was one wall that had a heater vent behind it, and I bent it out of shape. After I had gotten done snapping out, I went back to bed. I was wrong, so I had no other choice but to admit it. I erased the other woman's information from my cell phone, and after that, I didn't know how to get in touch with her. That was the end of that.

I still hadn't learned my lesson. I had many more pitfalls to come. My wife was also a cosmetologist, so we had things in common. I had gotten over us being equally yoked, as far as the church was concerned. We were adults so we would be fine. We had even decided that we would both become health conscious and stop eating beef and pork. We cleaned our systems out and started working out three to five times weekly. How awesome was this, I thought? This was a good plan. I had been going to McDonald's and ordering a Big Mac, a chicken sandwich, a fish sandwich, a Quarter Pounder, a cheeseburger, large french fries, and a large cup of water. I would eat every bit of it. I would also go to Harold's Chicken and order fourteen wings and two orders of fries and four cole slaws, and I didn't want to share. So, going on this health kick was good for me.

My wife and I had our differences, of course, but we would work through them. After some time had passed, a lady approached me about opening up a salon. I asked my wife what did she think, and she thought it sounded OK. So, we opened up a salon and it was very nice. I guess I was just an entrepreneur who wanted to have my own, and I didn't want my wife having to work for anyone. We had gained equity in our home, so we decided to sell and build our dream home. And we did just that. We sold our home and stayed with my grandmother until our home was completed. We were able to fully furnish every room in our home because we planned for it. I told my wife that I didn't want a big lavish home that was empty. It we couldn't furnish it, we would wait to buy it. We both agreed, and so we planned accordingly. Everything worked out in our favor. We built a home that had five bedrooms, four bathrooms, walk-in closets, a three-car garage, custom blinds to match the furniture in every room, an office, a theatre, and a music studio. The only thing I was adamant about having in our home was a gourmet kitchen with a commercial stove and a steam spa shower like the health club. Nothing else really mattered as much. You would have thought our house belonged on the MTV show *Cribs*.

I had just bought my second Navigator, and she had a Jaguar. Man, we had it going on, and the sky was the limit. I decided that I was starting to outgrow my barbershop on 103rd Street, and I was very fond of quite a few of the barbers. I told one of them that I wanted him to have it. The barber, whom I wanted to have the barbershop, and I settled on a price and I allowed him to pay me however it was feasible for him with no pressure. Even though I had another shop, I remained in the other location for an additional eight months to show I can follow as well as lead. I still treated the barbershop with respect as if I were still the owner, and that's the way it should be. I finally left and went to my other shop to work.

I wanted my wife and I to be able to build it up stronger. It was around 2002, and I decided that I wanted to go to my bank and tell them that I wanted to open up a barber college. I was very professional and had a business plan. Plus, I had four accounts with them, so I assumed I wouldn't have a problem getting a loan. I was wrong. They weren't going to give me a dime. Consequently, I pulled the money I had out of that bank and went to another bank to do business. I had refused to let anything stop me from any dreams and goals I had set, so I found another route to opening up my barber college.

Before I even knew where I was opening my barber college, I put all my major equipment in layaway, and paid on it every week. I was determined. I had faith, and I took a chance. I finally found a place where I could open up my college. It was across the street from the other barbershop on 103rd and Halsted Streets. Without anyone even telling me, I went and started a corporation. I wanted to be considered to be part of corporate America. The banks were so impressed that I went out on a limb, paid for everything and obtained a place to open my college, that they gave me a small credit line. I was ecstatic. It was only enough money to finish putting the place together but not enough to maintain my business for six months to a year.

I had just bought this big house, and we had these nice cars and a business to run. I had to make a decision. I talked to my wife and told her we could handle it and if we work hard. We could accomplish so much within the next few years. I had to start paying bills for the barber college before it had even opened, and I had to wait on the state to come out and inspect the college and approve it before I was able to except any students. In October 2004, the college finally opened. I was off and running. People started signing up like crazy. I had a staff to pay. I already had my barber's license. I was able obtain my teacher's license through my college, so I could minimize my overhead. Between our bills at home, the bills at the school and the salon, we spent between $18,000 to $21,000 monthly. My wife and I always worked together financially, so she would always give me about $3,000 every month to assist with paying the bills. I appreciated the help. A lot of times, couples don't work well together financially; however, I was still coming up short. So, I decided I would go to the casino. I learned how to play blackjack really well.

Now we were taught against gambling in church. I really wasn't supposed to be at the boat, but I felt as if gambling was the only way I could get funds to take care of my family. I had accepted my calling into the ministry, so I knew that wasn't right. I couldn't let anybody find out I was doing things against the teachings of the church. I would go to the casino and sometimes I would lose, and sometimes, I would win. I would see people sitting at the tables playing and winning tens of thousands of dollars and they were smoking, drinking, cursing, and having a good time. I was being judgmental. I felt that because they were the ones doing all the bad stuff, I should be winning instead of them. I would sit at the table and pray to God to please let me win. It didn't work. I knew I shouldn't have been there in the first place, but I wanted to be able to provide for my family. I would leave the casino furious. I would get mad at God because I felt as though he let the people who didn't care win in the casino, and I hadn't won much of anything. I would get so angry that I would drive home at 100 miles per hour constantly thinking of running my car over a cliff and killing myself. I would look at the news or read in the newspapers about people getting killed. I would be so envious of the people who had died because I felt like they were lucky not to have to deal with the struggles life had to offer. I wanted to go to sleep and never wake up again, so that everything

I was going through would go away. At this point, I wasn't afraid to die. If I were dead, the problems could no longer come my way. The spirit of suicide was very heavy on me, and the thought of it was almost uncontrollable. What made me always reconsider was the fact that I didn't want to leave my daughters without their father.

I went home, sat in my family room, and I stayed there in a state of depression. I cancelled all of my appointments at the barbershop because I was upset with everybody, whether they had done something or not. I took out my cell phone and started from A and went all the way to Z to ask for help. I got angry with everyone I had loaned or given money in the past but refused to repay me. I was messed up. I had no clue what was going on with me. Of course, I didn't think I had a problem.

My dad became the pastor at my grandmother's church, so we decided to go back and join my dad's church so that I could help him to go to the next level.

A year went by, and I decided that I was going to tell my dad that I had been molested as a child. When I told him, he was furious. He said that he told my mother that whenever I would come from over their friends' house, I wasn't the same. He said that I would have a rash, and they thought it was from wearing diapers. I told him I was alright and not to make a big deal out of it. Yet, I wasn't alright, and I still hadn't realized it. There was still something missing.

My wife and I started getting into altercations, and I couldn't figure out why. I was a great cook, so she always had hot breakfast as well as full-course dinners. I always made sure that snow was shoveled before she got home. The lawn was done, and I also did a excellent job of taking care of our daughter. I would get our daughter up for school almost every morning, and I would even sometimes cook her a full breakfast. If her mom wasn't home, I would make sure she got her homework done and was in bed by a reasonable time.

I was a very sexual man with my wife, so I didn't see where there could have been any problems in that area of our marriage. One of the things that could have been wrong was the fact that I had so many different experiences with so many women. I believe I had carried over baggage from other relationships with women. I concentrated more on trying to reach goals. I didn't realize that my wife didn't care about the same things. She was more concerned with having a balanced relationship with me. The communication was not there at all. We couldn't have a civilized conversation. We would be in the bed, and I would try to have a conversation with her. I felt as though I would have her undivided attention. I would often talk about things I needed closure on, and she refused to answer most of the questions. I was under the impression that a woman should tell a man, especially the one she loves, whatever he wants to know. With my wife, it wasn't like that. She very seldom said anything, and when she did, it would be something that hurt drastically. Still, I always went to sleep thinking positively and resolving the issues on my own.

I thought about leaving my dad's church and going to another church. I felt it would make things better because at a different house of worship, the preacher's message wouldn't be biased because it wouldn't be coming from my dad. I was hoping changing churches would help us, but it didn't. It just made us realize that we really weren't for each other.

What was going on with me? What was the use of continuing to live. I couldn't stay married. I'm a good guy. None of the things I was taught was coming to pass. Something was wrong. There were a lot of times when I really didn't feel loved by my wife, and she would tell me, "Of course I love you. Don't feel like that."

I just figured I would weather the storm again and wait for the happier years to come. I started feeling like something was wrong in some other areas of my marriage, so I started becoming really insecure, and I started thinking something was wrong with me.

I was blessed to have a special gift of discernment, and I could feel that things were going on, which caused me to have dream. I figured I was having the dreams because my wife would be at the shop late. I would want us to be able to spend time together, so I would always ask her what time she was coming home, and she would always seem like it bothered her to have to tell me. She would say she didn't know. She would say the reason that we can't spend time together was because I would always be asleep, but I was an early bird. I was up at 5 or 6 a.m. almost every day. She couldn't tell me a definite time when she was coming home, so I would fall asleep by 10 or 11 p.m. I would be asleep before she got home. I felt I had nothing to look forward to because I didn't know what time she was coming home.

She made me feel as though she wasn't rushing to get home, anyway, so it didn't matter. I believe that's why my dreams involved her and another man dating. I would wake up in a cold sweat and look over to see if she was in the house yet. She wouldn't be there. We had another room on the other side of the walk-through closet, and she would sometimes be in there exercising to one of her workout tapes.

One day, I was at the shop that I had opened for her. I felt as though we were mature enough to work in the same shop together without fighting, and it proved to be correct. I was standing up cutting hair, and my gut feeling told me to walk over to her station and look at her phone. She was in the back shampooing a client, so it was the perfect opportunity for me to look. It was unlike me to even engage in anything like that; however, I just had a feeling that I would get some information I really needed. As soon as I walked over to the phone, a text message came through. The text message read, "The cat must have your tongue; I know what has mine. I enjoyed myself last night, and I hope you did, too. I will see you when I get back in town."

My heart dropped. I didn't know what to do so I went back over to my station and continued to cut hair. I was determined to contain my composure, because I didn't want everyone in our business. I waited a while, and I called her into the back so I could talk to her. When we were alone, I produced her phone. I showed her what I saw, and I asked her to explain it. She said that it was a random text that she and her friends always get from people who send text messages for parties and such. So she didn't know who sent it. So I had her call the number. The guy on the other end knew something was up, so he was playing the dumb role. I remembered the number just in case it showed up again on her phone. I just told her it was OK. I believe her, and I just dropped the whole thing.

As time progressed, I continued to do everything I could to be a good husband and a father. Things pretty much remained the same, but I just assumed things would get better. I just endured it and felt as time passed, we would grow older and we would soon be a happy family. We had everything a family could imagine. I felt that was happiness in itself, but I had come to the realization true happiness was more than material things. I thought she was in love with me the same way I was in love with her. I figured we had to learn to live with one another. A lot of my friends are pastors, bishops and musicians who play for famous people, and I told one of my pastor friends that I was going to get up early and watch his broadcast one day.

I procrastinated watching, and one day, I remembered to tune in. I decided to go in the television room, which was through the walk-in closet. It had a door, so you could have some privacy. That was her haven at night where she would chill until she got ready to get in the bed and go to sleep. She would keep her phone plugged up in there as well. I went in and closed the door, and before I could even turn the television on, her phone started vibrating to alert her that she had a text message. Normally, she would turn her phone off. If it were turned back on, a code had to be put in to view numbers or messages. This particular night, she had to be waiting on someone to respond to her text because her phone was still on. The person responded after she had gone to bed.

Needless to say, I looked at the phone and the message said, "I love you, too. Have sweet dreams."

It was the same number I saw on her phone six months prior. My gift was working again, I thought. It was 6 a.m., and I went right in the bedroom and woke her up. I showed her the phone and told her that it was the same number from that day in the shop. She couldn't do anything but say, "OK, Larry."

She said he was one of her old boyfriends, and the two of them had been going out to a bar after work sometimes. I was livid. I said I knew it, and told her she had some explaining to do. She told me that she had enjoyed his company, and they would just have a drink from time to time. At this point, I'm figuring, OK. If I need to go to a bar with you, I would go because our marriage was very important to me, and I didn't want to lose her because she was afraid to let me know that there are things she enjoy doing that I don't care for. When I told her I would go out to a club with her and her friends or to a bar, she told me she realized that was not something that I enjoy doing, so she didn't want me to. So, at this point, I couldn't win for losing with her, I thought. I was willing to do anything it took to make sure our marriage evolved.

We got into a big altercation one day, which caused me to wild out. I had just come home from church on a Sunday, and I wanted to take a movie back that I had bought at the video store. We had driven two cars to church that day because I had to always be at church early so that I could set up the drums. This was during the summer, and she had to drop our daughter off at the skating rink, and I called her because I had some major concerns I just had to get off my chest. So I called her as I was leaving church. We talked all the way from 43rd Street and Drexel to 175th and Kedzie Street. I sat in the parking lot of the video store for awhile and finished talking to her. I decided that I didn't feel up to going in the video store, so I pulled out of the parking lot and decided to just go straight home. She said she had to go because she was tired of talking on the phone and she would talk to me later.

I decided to take a different route home. Not even five minutes had passed since our phone conversation, and I was sitting at the light on 183rd Street and Cicero, and my wife turned the corner at 183rd. I saw a guy in the car with her as I was sitting at the light. Then, I made a U-turn and I pulled up on the side of her car. I looked at her like what's going on, and she stopped her car, and I stopped my car. I got out of my car, and the dude got out of her car. My issue wasn't with him because I didn't know him. My issue was with her. She pulled off and left the dude on the side of the road, so I got back in my car and pulled off. She then reversed the car and let the guy back in the car. I was outdone.

She knew we weren't going to have a pleasant night, so she turned her phone off so I couldn't call her. I was sitting at home and her mom came over. After her mom got there, she showed up. I guess she wanted to make sure she had someone there so I would snap out. That was the day she decided to admit to me and her mom that she just wasn't in love with me anymore.

Later she was talking to me on the phone about getting divorced, and this guy had to have been in the car, but she insisted he wasn't. I didn't believe her story, but again like a dummy, I went along with it. Her mom and I asked her who the guy in the car was. She said this guy was someone who ran out of gas in the parking lot of the bowling alley and he needed her to take him home to get his gas can so he could go to the gas station. The first question I had was, why would you pick up a total stranger especially a man? It didn't make sense. I also told her that there was a gas station in the parking lot of the bowling alley, which was a grocery store. What sense did it make for you to take a total stranger, "who could have been a killer," across town to his house to get a $5 gas can that he could have purchased at the gas station or even the grocery store?

At this point I needed some answers, so without letting my daughter know what was going on, I asked her if she knew anything about the situation. Her mom said that it was one of her friend's uncles who had run out of gas. The story changed so much, I didn't know what to believe. By this time, everything started getting revealed to me, and it seemed as though I knew exactly where to go, when to go, what to do, and when to do it. I didn't want my marriage to be over, so I was willing to do whatever I needed to do in order to save my marriage, but for some reason I started feeling like God was giving me the door to escape, but I didn't know how to. So, I remained for another three weeks. Those were the worst three weeks I could ever have in my life. I went downtown to cut one of my celebrity client's hair, and I got done earlier than I had anticipated. So, I decided that I would go back out to the suburbs, and I called my wife to tell her I was on my way home. She said she was going to the health club before she picked up my daughter from the bus stop. I decided to go the health club and meet her there. I parked right in the front when I had spotted her car. I used my key to unlock the door to make sure it was her car, and at this point, I was looking for any evidence that something was going on. She had decided that she was looking for somewhere to move to, so she had a lot of items from different apartment buildings in the car. I went up to the front desk and had them to page her, and they called her over the intercom three times. She never responded, so they told me she must not be there. There was only one way in and one way out, besides the emergency doors. I walked outside and noticed this guy on a cell phone, and I caught his eye as well. It appeared to be the same guy I caught in the car with her, so he turned away, but I didn't think about it anymore until I noticed her car was gone. There was no way possible that she could have been able to get by me inside the health club without me seeing her. I'm figuring that she and this guy were in the car watching me or they went somewhere together in his car, and he dropped her back off.

I had to get down to the bottom of it. When I approached her, she said that wasn't the same guy that was in the car. That guy was her trainer from the health club. I knew I wasn't going crazy. I would never forget how this guy who had been in her car looked, so I knew for a fact it was him.

I felt as though I had been deceived. She would always rush off to the health club, but I now felt he was the reason why.

I told her if she were not honest with me, I would go home and bust out all of the windows and mess up all of our expensive furniture. At this point, I needed some answers as to why we weren't able to be happy. I knew I hadn't done anything wrong. The police were called, and when they arrived, I told them that this is my house and I could do whatever I pleased. My dad and my wife's mom and stepdad came over. The police left because they knew my dad and they knew me from having my barbershop in Matteson.

We all sat at the table, and I was crying like I was losing my mind, and she was sitting up like nothing was bothering her. I couldn't take it anymore, so I decided I was going to snap out. My dad had just had a double-bypass surgery. He grabbed me, and at this point, I wasn't thinking about me anymore. I was concerned about my dad not hurting himself. He wouldn't let me go, so I pulled away, and I punched the granite countertop in my kitchen, and my hand and my fingers turned black, blue, and purple.

My mother in law was crying and upset because she didn't understand what was going on. After everything had calmed down later that evening, my mom arrived with my dad and asked me what was really going on. They were so used to me always throwing clippers at people in the shop and beating people up, they automatically assumed it was something I did.

In 2004, I reiterated to my mom and dad that I had been molested which is part of why there was so much going on with me. He told me that he told my mother when I was little that something wasn't right and he couldn't figure out what would be wrong with me when I would come from over their friend's house.

I told him I was fine with his not knowing what happened to me, and I went and had counseling. Most of my hurt was from the fact that I felt as though my parents never listened to me. I lived a forced way of life, and because I lived like that, I felt like the only way to succeed was to live like I was taught. Therefore, these teachings made me judgmental, and I had a one-track mind. I thought if I lived a perfect life, I wouldn't have any problems along the way. I told them that I wasn't upset that we were brought up in a very positive loving environment, but I didn't know how to relax when times got tough. I thought that living a perfect life meant that I wouldn't have any problems. I poured my heart out to my parents that day, and had them listen to me for a change.

I expressed to them that it has always been if there was a problem, it was swept under the carpet and never dealt with. We had to do what they said, and that was final. I explained to them that I was molested and that was serious. And their reply was that, we told you if anybody ever touched you or bothered you to let us know. I explained to them that when you are a kid, you don't know the difference between what's right and what's wrong. The truth of the matter was, I was threatened by my molester. He assured me that if I said anything, he would beat me. I use to get punched in my chest really hard as a small child to show the repercussion of telling anything that went on. Besides, how could you think something is wrong when you are being taught by the person that it's OK? This had a serious affect on me because I started growing up, and I had feelings inside of me that I needed to express, but I didn't know how or if I was supposed to even express them. Every time we went to visit relatives or the home of friends, I always found myself wanting to play house with the girls because I wanted to be able to express my feelings due to what I had been taught. This wasn't right but I didn't know that, so I continued to act out in this manner every time I got a chance. In my eyes, the good thing about it is that even though a teenage male molested me, I knew that man and man weren't suppose to be together. I had a great father figure and good strong uncles who surrounded me and they portrayed how men should be. I knew that a man is supposed to be with a woman.

When I went to counseling while my second marriage was failing, I had learned that I was a womanizer. By this time, I had slept with close to four hundred women. Still, I didn't think I had any problems. I just figured I had a way with women. What I didn't realize was that I was trying to prove to myself that I was a real man; however, if I would have gotten help earlier, then I wouldn't have gone down this road. I didn't realize because of what I had gone through, I also acted out and I was always angry and mad at the world. I thought I had forgiven him in my heart, but I hadn't because I wasn't healed and free from it all. When I dug the issue up, I had to destroy it so it would never come back to haunt me anymore, which has now caused me to be able to tell someone else what I went through. How does a child understand something if no one explains it thoroughly? I was the best husband I could possibly be, and I worked hard the same way I had seen my father work all my life. I am always good to people, whether they like me or not. I will help anyone who needs help. I have paid car notes and mortgages for friends and family members. I've bought them clothes and fulfilled other financial needs. I even did these things sometimes for people when I couldn't even do for myself, but I figured I was strong and I knew how to brave the storm because I was a survivor. I've had so many clients who would come in to get a service and they either couldn't pay or needed credit, and I gave it to them. They didn't know that I was up against the wall. Some of these same people today see my struggles and know that my heart is pure. I'm only trying to reach the point of riches so that people around me far and near can benefit. I felt that some people around me did not want to see me succeed and that hurt very badly. We should all want to see other people be successful.

Later on that night, my wife and daughter went and spent the night at her mom's house because there was too much tension between us. I fell asleep in the television room. I woke up at about 12:45 a.m., and I went into the bedroom to go to sleep. The phone was right by my head, and it rang. I normally don't answer the phone, but I did on this particular occasion, and it was my wife.

I was excited because I thought she had called to reconcile but I found out that she accidentally called the house without knowing she had dialed home. She and some guy were talking about how stupid I looked peeping into her car earlier at the health club and how I was a damn fool. I listened to them laugh and talk about me long enough and decided to hang up and tried to call her back. She didn't answer the phone, so I called over to her mom's house and her stepdad answered the phone, and I asked him if I could speak to her, and he said she wasn't there. I went on to tell him what had just transpired. She came walking through the door and got on the phone. After that, I told her what happened. She claimed she didn't know what I was talking about, so I told her to look at her phone to see she accidentally called. She claimed that the guy was someone else, and not the dude I thought he was. It was my imagination. She said she had just gone out to have a drink to calm her nerves. At this point, I was really hurting, but I didn't care. I just wanted to do what needed to be done in order to save my marriage.

CHAPTER 9

DON'T GIVE UP

I cried out, and people didn't even realize it.

I cried out to my wife that I love her, but she said, "I'm not in love with you anymore."

I knew I was a good man. I hadn't done anything wrong. I'd made so many sacrifices, and my wife's love faded away. What was I suppose to do? I wanted to go to counseling. She said, "Larry, a counselor can't change the way I feel."

I thought about it, and she was right. A counselor could only be a mediator. I said, "Let's start all over from the beginning and date again."

"I don't want to date again," she said.

I said, "Let's write down all of our likes and dislikes."

"I don't want to do that," she replied.

I had tried everything I could do, and nothing was working. I started thinking it was me, which made me begin searching myself. I would go in the bathroom and look in the mirror. Maybe I was ugly to her. I assumed that since some of her friends had husbands who could give them the world, I would go to the casino even more so that I could not only be a man and take care of all the bills, but also buy her anything she wanted. I ended up losing more money and further messing things up. I figured I would try and impress her by letting her know I had major plans for our future. It didn't work. I finally realized that it wasn't me personally; some people just grow apart and aren't meant for each other.

I cried for three weeks straight. I didn't eat for three days at a time, and I lost a lot of weight. When I wasn't at church or work, I was cooped up in the house in a depressive state. We had built our big, beautiful dream house, and I had just opened up my first barber college. This couldn't be happening to me. My life was over, I thought.

"Let's just get separated for a while," my wife said.

I figured why prolong it? Who wants to live in a house where there is tension? It wouldn't be good for us. It could be a dangerous situation, and my daughter would suffer. I sat my daughter on my lap and explained to her that her mom and dad were going to part, and that no matter what, I was going to continue being the best father to her. She cried her eyes out, and I was crying, too. She understood as best as she could. I didn't talk negatively about her mom because that's not what this was about. She needed to know that she could love her mom and dad equally, even though our relationship didn't work out.

Here I go again. I loaded up my things. I gave some items away to teenagers who were growing and needed clothes and shoes. I moved in with a friend, and I had to sleep on a pallet on the floor for two months until he had to sell his place. I was forced to either go and sleep at my barber college or try and find someone who could take me in. At this point, I figured that I was of no use to this world. I was failing, so why should I even be living? I wanted to just die and be gone, so I wouldn't have to worry about dealing with the unfair pressures of life, as I called them.

I decided that maybe it would be best for me to sell my barber college and move out of the state and start all over, but I didn't want to leave my daughter and my nephews. I decided against that. I had nothing: no money, no place to live, no wife, and no stability. I was doomed. Life just wasn't worth living.

A young lady called me and said, "I heard you were getting divorced."

"Yes," I said.

"What's up?" she said. "Let's hook up."

I was like, "Cool!"

So we did. She also helped me get an apartment in Lake Meadows, where I had once resided. I made enough money for the security deposit, so I was cool. I paid all of the bills at my home, so she just had to rent the apartment for me because I was going through the divorce, and my credit had started to look bad. She let me borrow her television, microwave, and some mattresses, so I could be comfortable, and I was appreciative. In 2006, I started getting back into some real-estate ventures that allowed me to make some extra money, so I was feeling a little better. The extra income still wasn't enough because my college started falling to pieces. I had to default on a couple of business credit lines from the bank because my wife and I were no longer together, so it was either I keep my bills at the college paid, along with my car note and apartment or pay the credit lines. They froze my accounts and took what they wanted, which left me trying to recoup my losses.

I didn't have any outside credit cards. They were all tied to my business line of credit.

I did have a wonderful college, but students couldn't sign up because my financial aid program hadn't started yet. I had quite a few students, but everybody wasn't always able to pay the tuition. I didn't want to kick anyone out, so I worked with them because I figured I needed them just like they needed me. I had a lot of guys who were in my college because they wanted to change their lives, and I believed I could help them succeed. With everything going on, I never slighted my students or anyone else when it came to doing what I was obligated to do. I always smiled, taught and cut hair, and anything else I had to do without fail.

I had students come to me and say, "Mr. Roberts, if you would have kicked me out and not given me a chance, I probably would have been back out on the streets hustling or in jail somewhere."

At that moment, nothing I was going through mattered because I realized that my ministry was in helping people to get to their next level. I felt like the struggle was worth it. Also, I was willing to go through the next stages. You have to have your college open for at least two years before you can start the application process. I still had to pay $10,000 in order to go through the process. How was I going to do that?

All of my students couldn't pay out-of-pocket. How does a school pay almost $25,000 a month in expenses, if it can't accept financial aid for the students who need it in order to attend? I'm really up to my head in everything that is going on, and at this point, I can't believe any of this. WHY WAS ALL OF THIS HAPPENING TO ME?

My lady friend saw me going through all of this, and she decided we were in this together, and she wanted to help. She decided to take out a few loans to help me. I agreed that I would pay them back monthly. We were both fine with the arrangement. What a great woman I had! I had also given her money to meet other needs, and I was buying her a lot of things. I paid for food and most of our events. We did things for one another equally. After a while, things weren't going so well with me and my lady, so I decided that it was best that we part. I called her over and we talked. It was a hard breakup, but I felt that it was necessary. I continued to fulfill my obligation at the apartment, even though my name wasn't on the lease. I didn't want to leave anything outstanding. I found a place that a friend was rehabbing. I put a bid in for one of his condos, and he accepted. I had to wait until it was completed.

I felt as if I had to be with a woman, so I found another lady friend, and we started dating. I eventually became very fond of her. My other lady found out, and it was all hell from that point. She wanted me out of the apartment, but I wasn't going to move until my other place was ready. Needless to say, I ended up moving out, but I made sure I didn't leave any outstanding bills. I did still need to pay off the loans she had gotten for me, but since they were for the college, I had my sister, who was the administrator, put it in the budget for her to get paid monthly.

We didn't have a formal contract; this agreement was formed because we had been a couple and she wanted to help. I told her that I would pay the loans, so that's what I did. I dated this other young lady for awhile, but she still wasn't who I was looking for. She and I decided to go our separate ways. One of the things I admired most about this young lady was that she was very supportive, which made it hard for me not to want to be with her. There were times when I thought I was losing my mind. I was crying like a baby because this didn't need to be happening to a good person like me. She would come and read me scriptures from the Bible and pray for me. She wiped the tears from my eyes and let me know, "Weeping may endure for a night, but joy comes in the morning."

But again I was searching for something more, and I couldn't really put my hand on it. I felt that I was continuing to fail. Then, I started dating one of the most beautiful, smartest women I had ever met in my life. Is this it, I'm thinking? The young lady who had taken out the loans for me, found out I was dating someone she knew, and she totally went ballistic. She started denying that she had received the payments from my sister, and decided that she wanted the payment in full. Of course I couldn't pay her the money in full because I had businesses to run, and when I was able to pay her in full I would. That wasn't good enough for her. She was upset, and she decided she was going to take me to court. To add insult to injury, she gained my wife's job information and called her and told her everything that was going on, as if I hadn't already told my wife. Everything was OK with our payment arrangement until I decided to marry again for the third time. Right after I had gotten married, I received papers to go to court one month later. My wife didn't feed into the mess; it was hilarious to her. This woman did everything she could to defame me, which I felt was unfair, but what do you do. We went to court and wasted all of that time. The judge took us right back to the original payment arrangement, which proved that I was doing everything right from the beginning.

People who I've done business with knew me, so they knew I was honest, but it seemed as if I was lying sometimes. I made promises to people based on the promises I was made from the financial institutions. I was made promises that didn't come through a lot of times from the financial institutions. Five grant writers took my money and promised me that I would get more than $850,000, but it never happened. There were bankers who promised me that if I paid them a certain amount of money, they could turn the tables and clear up my credit lines and get me more. That never happened. There were people who came to the negotiation table with me on a deal, and they dropped out, so the deal never happened. Wow! What do I do? I was trying everything I could to be an overcomer and accomplish my goals, but it just isn't working out. I am an award-winning barber and on top of that, my students were winning awards through my school. I have instructional DVDs out on the market, and I even started my own product line. I NEED HELP, AND NO ONE WOULD HELP ME!!!

CHAPTER 10

It Is Not The End

It Is Not The End

I was tired of going through it all, and I was tired of living in this world. I don't sleep at night because I'm too stressed. I don't have any money, and I feel like my family wasn't able to help me. If my family couldn't help me, then who could?

I would be standing up cutting hair, and I would feel myself getting ready to have a stroke. I believe God kept me. I would feel like I was getting ready to pass out while holding the clippers in my hand. They were trying to repossess my truck. I wanted to voluntarily return it and ride the bus, but I would have had to still pay for it. I just let it reach a 45-day status, then I had planned to send a MoneyGram to pay it before they came to repossess it. I felt as though taking care of my daughter, my college and having a place to live was more important.

One day, I got a call from the local television station telling me that they want me to be featured on the program *Someone You Should Know* with Harry Porterfield. Oh, man.

Was I excited. They came out to film the show, and I was seen all over Chicago. It was one of the best days ever.

I had never had a relationship with my oldest daughter, but I discovered she was in *Who's Who* in Columbus, Ohio. A family member said that it was a coincidence that her daddy was on Someone You Should Know, and she was in *Who's Who*. They reached out to me and gave me a number to call if I wanted to so. I did, and boy was I happy. After fifteen years, I finally had a chance to make the acquaintance of my oldest daughter.

I figured in time it would happen. That's why I made sure that any woman I had ever been with knew that one day my oldest daughter was going to be in my life. I wanted them to accept her, which they did. I flew out to see my daughter that following week, and it made me so happy. We slowly started to build a really strong, healthy relationship. It was a little rocky at first, but it all started to come together. Who could blame her? She really didn't know what was going on or where I was, but after we talked, she understood. I said to myself, "I believe everything is going to be alright. Suicide Is Not The Answer to my problems."

Not long after that, I became really sick. I was sicker than I had ever been in my life. I had blood in my urine for three weeks. I had to urinate about fifteen times every day, and it felt like a million needles were trying to come out. I wouldn't wished this on my worst enemy. I would actually be in tears every single time I went to the restroom.

The doctors didn't know what was going on with me. They thought I had a kidney stone that I was trying to pass, but that wasn't the problem. One doctor checked me for cancer, and that wasn't it. It wasn't until I went to a specialist that my cousin, who is a nurse, referred me to, who gave me some pills that slowly knocked all the pain out. Each time after that, when I went to the rest room, I said, "Thank you, God for allowing me to be able to urinate." It's the small things we do daily that we sometimes take for granted.

I was approached by a lady to begin a barber school and a beauty school. I didn't have any money, so I wasn't sure how was I going finance such a business endeavor.

"Well if it's meant for me to have then the money will be provided," I said.

Wouldn't you know that right when it was almost too late, I made agreements with a few people to put up money to become a part of this growing corporation. So, I ended up opening up another barber college and a beauty college. How could all of this happen with all of the problems I'm having. The saying goes, "It's a poor dog that won't wag his own tail."

So I always spoke highly about my business because I knew that one day all of the trials and tribulations would become limited, and I would be a successful millionaire or even billionaire.

I would be able to pass on my legacy and open colleges and high-end salons and spas all over the world. I had already begun my own product line, which included a full line of hair care products along with bump therapy products for men and women.

In writing this book, I've established that people often

say they want to commit suicide as a means of getting attention. We want people to hear us, but it seems as if telling them isn't good enough because our problems are not important to them. We want people to feel our pain because we feel if they feel our pain, they would come to our rescue. We want people to wish they could have done something to stop us from killing ourselves. We want people to mourn us after we are gone. But when we're gone, they are going to mourn for a while and then move on with their lives. For me, suicide would have been a way for the people close to me to talk about what could have been done to prevent it. I wasn't really aware of that though. I had often imagined what my funeral would be like. I wanted validation, so I figured everyone would say a bunch of good stuff about me. What good would it have done if I could not hear or receive what the people had to say? But this was all nonsense. I want to live.

I found my true love, and I couldn't have been a happier man. Besides my mother, she is the greatest woman who I've ever known. She is the true meaning of what it means to be a good wife, mom, lover, helpmate and everything else that defines true love. We live to make one another happy, and we have formed a circle that we won't allow anybody to violate.

In 2008, my wife and I had been married for eight months, and I just knew that everything was going to be alright. She was there for me through some of the toughest times of my career, but she didn't let it faze her. She kept pushing and crying for me and crying with me when I didn't think I could endure anymore. She told me that we would look back on this day and laugh about it.

My lease was up on my truck, which was my third Lincoln Navigator, and it was time for me to get another car. I'd paid a car note that ranged from $1,000 to $1,300 since I was twenty-two years old. It was time to do something different, but my pride was getting in the way. I was accustomed to driving whatever kind of car I wanted to drive and whatever I had to pay for it was not an issue, but I was starting to understand that realistically, I couldn't afford expensive cars. I had bought a Ford Explorer for my daughter who I had reconnected with. She was 16 years old, and one of the most exciting things I did for her was to buy her a car and drive it to Columbus as a surprise. I bought the car with cash, so I took the title and transferred it to her state in order to get the insurance together. I went to her school and surprised her with it. Some weeks had gone by, and she had a few complications, so she decided she wanted to leave home. When she left home, of course, it voided the insurance. I had no other choice at the time but to go back and get the car. My wife flew to where she was and drove the car back for me, since my schedule didn't allow me to go. It couldn't wait, so we didn't waste any time. I would be liable for anything that happened with the car.

I got the car back, and I wasn't driving it. Every now and then I would drive it, but it just sat in front of the house. It was time for me to turn my car in, so I had to decide if I was going to keep it or get a new car. I wanted a new car, so keeping it wasn't an option for me because my pride had me thinking I was too good to keep that car. I wanted another

Range Rover. A brand new Range Rover was going to cost me $85,000. To lease it for three years would require that I put down almost $10,000 because my credit wasn't the best. I was determined to get a new car, so by any means necessary (of course legally), I was going to get a new truck. I could hardly pay my bills at my businesses. When I had my other truck, I had to alternate my bills with my car note every month. After thinking about that, I had a reality check. I looked outside and I said, "I have a car that I paid cash for that cost me $75 a month for full coverage. How crazy would I be to go out and buy a car that I couldn't afford at the time?"

I swallowed my pride, and I got in that Explorer and drove it. At first, I was embarrassed. Not because it was a bad car, but because I felt like I've always driven the best cars. I had a brand new Eddie Bauer Ford Explorer when I was twenty-four years old, so I didn't want to go backward. That was beneath me. When I would go places, I didn't want people to know I was driving the car, so I would park where no one could see me. I came to myself soon after. That was the point at which I felt as if I had matured for real this time. Who cared what I was driving? I had multiple businesses, and I was putting myself in a position where I might not have been driving around in a car. I couldn't afford faking and shaking like so many other people. I held my head high, and I drove the wheels off of that car. Something happened with the front lock and the electrical system. In order to unlock the front door, I would have to open the back door and reach in the front and open the door by hand. Some times the battery would die, and I couldn't get in the car. At least once a month, I would have to call the tow truck company and have the technician jimmy my car open and give me a jump. I would sit back in unbelief and ask, "God, what did I do to have to go through all of this?"

But I kept pushing, not knowing that people were looking at me as I was helping people from a distance. Someone said to me, " Larry, man I just want to say that your swag is so dope until it doesn't matter what you drive. It doesn't change who you are." That was one of the most amazing statements ever made to me. It really made me hold my head up and square my shoulders and strive harder to put everything in perspective.

Time went by and I had been communicating with my daughter off and on. She was going through a phase in her life, and I didn't know how to help her. I always treated her the same way as I treated my other daughter. There were no big I's and little U's. I was fair and loving across the board. She was seventeen years old, and I told her it was time for us to take a blood test for both of our sanity. I also felt like if I was going to be doing everything a father does to make sure that his children are protected, it was only right to find out if she's my blood daughter. We had been separated for about fifteen years due to earlier misunderstandings. When the test results came back, it was noted in detail that there was a 99.9% chance that she was not my daughter. This was one of the most hurtful things ever. I had only been with her mom that one time, but all it takes is one time, and this was the only way we were able to find out. I called her and shared the news. I also told her I didn't care what the test said. I was still going to be a father to her and not treat her any differently and help her find her real dad. She decided that she didn't want to find him. She wanted me to continue being her dad, and I agreed. My daughter called me later and said she had spoken to her biological mother, who basically told her that she had already known I wasn't her father. This explained why when the baby was born, her family did not want to consent to a blood test. That was so unfair!

I still did my part in contacting her, but she got a little sidetracked and would rarely respond to me, so it pretty much destroyed the relationship we had established. It was beyond my control. She would contact me if she needed something, which was to be expected. I had helped her in the past, but I felt it was somewhat unfair that I was only contacted when something was needed. I told her this, and we formed an understanding. That was taken care of, but more trials and tribulations would come. It just never stopped.

My cable had already been off for two months, but it was cool because that wasn't a necessity. Then my wife's mom was having complications with her landlord, and he wouldn't fix the heat, so she had to live in her apartment without any heat. I couldn't believe it because she was one of the sweetest women in the world, plus she had a daughter, and they didn't deserve to live like that. Being the type of person I was, I decided that she could move in with us, and I wasn't taking no for an answer. She said OK. Even though there was not enough room I wanted her to be OK and have peace of mind. My wife and I decided to join the health club together to work out. We felt as though it would assist us in the morning to shower and get ready for work at the club, so four adults wouldn't be trying to get ready in the morning at the same time. As soon as we got our health club memberships, the heat was shut off in my entire building. The gas company told us that even though it wasn't any fault of ours, in order for them to come and turn the gas back on, we would have to pay the entire bill. I didn't know what we were going to do because it was still cold outside, and there was no hot water. My wife cried until she couldn't cry anymore because she felt as much good that we did for others, we couldn't catch a break for anything in the world. Why did this have to happen to us? We were good people and hard workers, and we just wanted to be able to live on a day-to-day basis, but for some reason, we just couldn't get a break.

Even though her mom and sister hadn't moved in yet, we had no other choice but to go to the health club every day, even on Sundays before church, to take showers and get ready for the day ahead. It was weird having to wash up in cold water when at home, and we had to stay out of the house until bedtime almost. It was too cold to sit in the house. The only way we were able to stay warm was to get in the bed and snuggle together underneath the comforters. We dreaded getting up in the morning because it was a pain getting up in a freezing cold house to get ready. Still, we laughed about it and we continued on as if nothing was even wrong. One thing I can say about my wife, is that it didn't bother her at all because she said we were in this together. What a dream come true!

How do I go day after day helping people, and I can't even get anyone to help me? It's too hard to have to think about because it just seems as if everyone in the world should love one another enough to make sure we are all able to get along. Unfortunately, not everyone thinks that way. Where do I go from here? I am a business owner of three colleges. I have my own haircare product line. I'm in the process of opening up salons and more schools, and I believe God enough to realize that what I'm going through is only temporary because as Bishop Larry D. Trotter says, "What's To Come Is Betta Than What's Been." I truly believe that things are already looking better for me.

I went through all of this suffering, and felt like I had it together. I was on my way when I suddenly hit the lowest point of depression of my entire life. People were calling me and pulling on me, wanting this and needing that. I felt as though no one was willing to give me what I needed. It's not good to sit or lie around and think about things you are going through. Sometimes, you end up being in a state that is very difficult to come out of. I had a day where I could not stop thinking about all I was going through and all the people who I felt left me to fail. I lost the desire to live. I became overwhelmed with this entire burden, so I cried out to my wife and my sister and told them I was tired and I instructed them on how to handle all of the business, so no one would be left out. They didn't take me seriously, but I was serious. I took some pills in an amount that exceeded the dosage on the bottle, and then I got in the bed to die. I sent a text to my wife and told her what I had done, and she left her job very anxious to get to me. She put out some calls to my family and friends because she wanted someone to come see about me. I felt myself falling to sleep when I heard someone beating on my door. I thought I was hearing things, but I gathered up enough strength to go and see who was at the door. It was Pastor John Hannah and Pastor Tim. My wife had called them.

"Put your clothes on," said Pastor Tim. "I'm taking you to the hospital." I told him I didn't need to go, but I was stumbling and was very drowsy, so he insisted, and I did. My dad called Pastor Hannah to find out where he was taking me. He, as well as my wife and mother-in-law, came up to the hospital. The ER was very crowded but they were able to take me in right away. They made me drink two cups of a liquid called tar, and it was the worst. The medicine would overtake the pills I took. I couldn't believe I was almost out of here. Then I thought to myself, "What good would I have been to anyone if I had died?" I started thinking about my family, my students and all the people who need me around. I figured God had given me another chance at life, and this time I wasn't going to turn back. There are too many people's destinies linked to me, and I can't give up. I must keep striving. NO TEST, NO TESTIMONY!!! I was in ER all day long because they had to draw a lot of blood and take a lot of test before they transported me over to the other hospital. I had never in my life been in an ambulance, but I definitely experienced being in one that day. They took me up to a special part of the hospital, and I just thought it was a normal procedure, but they actually took me to the psychiatric ward. I was confined to a secure part of the hospital. I became aware of where I was after they informed my wife of what I could and could not have while I was there. She was also told when she would be able to visit me. I was in a part of the hospital where there were people with different issues that were considered a chemical imbalance in the brain. I immediately knew that I did not belong in this ward, so I started asking about what was really going on. Needless to say, they were limited things they could really tell me because I hadn't seen the doctor yet, and they didn't want to alarm me. I had no clothes or anything; just a hospital gown, which was unusual for me because I had never spent the night in a hospital. I had to adjust as best as I possibly could. There was only a television in the lounge area, and it went off at 10 p.m. I had to go to my room and meditate, and luckily I didn't have to share rooms with anyone because I was already uncomfortable. The nurse came in very early that next morning to draw more blood and also take my blood pressure. Immediately following her was the doctor who came in to make sure that I was physically fit and my liver wasn't damaged. People who overdose on pills can end up with liver damage, which of course can be very deadly. Overdosing on pills along with any other form of suicide was now definitely out of the question for me. Even if you survive the attempt, you could damage your body or organs for life. Well, thank God I was healthy. This made me and the doctor feel at ease. Then the psychiatrist came in following the medical doctor because he wanted to find out what got me to the point of suicide. There were a lot of things I could have said, but I narrowed it down to stress, which disturbed him because he didn't understand why I was in the mental state I was in. He stated that I was a good business owner and I was well liked. I also had an awesome wife, beautiful children and a wonderful family as a support system. I just told him that I was at a point where I was very overwhelmed, and it was just more than I felt like I could bear. I believe in God, and I am a believer now that He would not put more on you than you can bear.

The psychiatrist said that he would consider putting me on some medicine, and he asked me if I currently took any medicine. I told him I have never taken anything other than regular medicine for normal problems every blue moon. He wanted to base his decision on whether he thought I was bipolar or a hypomaniac. I knew I wasn't either one of those things, so I had already decided that I wasn't taking any medicine under any circumstance. I told the doctor the only medicine that I needed was seven figures wired to my bank account, and I guaranteed him that any problem he thought might be there would go away immediately. Realistically, money is not everything. I had to realize that I was rich in family and love, so I took another perspective on the way I thought about things. I learned how to just take one day at a time, and make the best of it. I would stop worrying about things that hadn't happened yet. Once I started looking at things differently, I was able to take control mentally. Being there in that part of the hospital, I had no choices in the matter. I had to follow all of the rules and regulations. After we were through eating breakfast, we were obligated to go to group therapy and talk about things that were going on with us. We had to go and draw pictures and do different things, and I told my wife this was definitely a place I didn't belong in.

Not living anymore seemed like the best resolution for a situation like mine, because if I were no longer in the land of the living, I wouldn't have to deal with all of these ups and downs. I figure that I had to die someday anyway, so I could expedite the process because I couldn't face tomorrow. I never wanted my days to end because I knew that the next day would bring another set of problems I didn't want to have to deal with. I'm glad that I had family members who didn't give up on me. I had a beautiful wife and children to live for. If I were to lose everything material, it wouldn't be the end of the world. I would just have to pick up and start all over again. My main problem was not wanting anyone to think that I was a liar or a cheater because I had not been able to come through on some of the promises I had made. I believe that everyone knew that I was an honest person, but the way things worked were out of my control. The economy had gotten bad, which meant it was rough for everyone, but the good thing was that no matter how bad things became, people were always going to find money to get their hair fixed or cut and have their nails done, so I always felt as though my career was protected and would never be taken for granted. I looked forward to training many more people through my colleges, and I knew that my day was coming to be able to open locations all over the world and also to mentor young men and women. I have a whole lot to live for.

CHAPTER 11

My Marriage Started
TO FAIL FOR THE THIRD TIME

My current marriage, which I thought was doing so well, had started to go down the drain, and I couldn't understand it. MY THIRD MARRIAGE?? There's always two sides to the story, and I will never claim to have been perfect, but I'm going to share my side of the story. Age is nothing but a number, and I'm holding firm to that because I don't think its meant for me to be with someone my age or older, specially because I'd love to have more children. My wife was nine years younger than me, and I felt like it mattered only regarding lack of experience in certain areas. I would be lying if I didn't say she was an amazing young lady because she is very much so, but the timing for us to be together was off. Personally speaking, if people haven't experienced certain things, they could ruin a perfectly good situation and not know it. For example, before you get married, especially these days, travel first and see the world so you can know what's out there. Before you get married, you should make sure you are getting married for the right reasons. That's the first thing. Check out the person's background and his or her immediate family to see what's in the bloodline. See if the person's mother or father was around and if they played an intricate part in the person's life as a child. Make sure that a person is financially sound, and if they aren't financially sound make sure they understand what it would take in order to get there. If a person is not happy with himself or herself, then they could never ever make you happy. Sometimes, we realize these things when it's too late. When this happens, you risk a perfectly good chance to have a successful marriage. Of course, no relationship is going to be perfect, but when things start coming out that you were unaware of and you thought it was one way and it ends up being different, it could cause problems that could very well be difficult to solve, in some cases.

My third wife was very supportive, more than I could ever imagine a woman being to me. Considering I was capable of taking care of myself, I was accustomed to being self-sufficient. There were minimal things I required in my marriage, but I didn't limit my wife from being as good of wife as she wanted to be. The things I required were normal things that a husband would expect from his wife, so it was nothing out of the norm. There were many things that transpired in my marriage. In the beginning, I just chalked it up as being a part of a learning curve and growing together; however, as the years went by, I thought about the fact that how certain things made me feel like less of a man, and they were being repeated.

There was a particular building I wanted for the location of my next barber college. I prayed over it and claimed it. I called the building's owner to ask him how much he wanted for it and what I needed to do to occupy it. He was very nice each time. I let him know that my plan was to put my barber college in the building. I told him the building was my building, and I was claiming it. He just kinda said, "Yeah OK, buddy. Anyway, first come first serve." Still, I kept calling and kept believing that this was my building. I would notice that sometimes when I called, he would seem a little frustrated. There was no indication as to whether I was going to get the building or if I was just calling and wasting his time.

One day I called, and he said, "Can I help you?" I told him that I had $10,000 to put toward buying the building. When I said that, he suddenly changed his tone and met with me. He said I have to come up with most of the rest of the money in order to do a complete build out to the building. The next time I met with him, I had another $10,000, but he wouldn't start the process until I had about $50,000. I was trying to figure out how I was going to run my day to day business for the two colleges that I already had, but God allowed me to be disciplined enough to maintain my businesses as well as save up the money to get my new building up and running. All of this was going on during the same time I was fighting to save my marriage. I hated speaking negatively, but I kept feeling like I wanted to get divorced because it was too much for me to deal with my wife and me not seeing eye to eye and trying to succeed in business.

Just when I thought I didn't have anyone really supporting me, I had a few people who believed in me enough to help me out. They invested a little money into my business. Let's just call it a loan I had to pay back. The banks wouldn't give me the money I needed. They only wanted to offer me enough money to fail, in my opinion, and when they did give loans, they wanted you to sign your life away. I wasn't willing to do that because if I would have borrowed the little money they were willing to give me, there was a possibility that I may have defaulted again. Since the loan amount wasn't enough to complete the project. My ex-wife's grandmother, "God rest her soul," was very instrumental in helping us gain the leverage we needed to make some things happen. For that, I will be forever grateful.

There were many times when I felt as though God wasn't hearing me, and He just wasn't there for me. Then I had to rethink that. Every time I didn't think I was going to get through a situation, God always showed up just in the nick of time. This amazed me. So, time went on, and it seemed like I was experiencing the most hell I'd ever experienced in my life. and it didn't seem fair. I finally got the building I'd worked so hard to buy, but I couldn't put all of the money together that I needed in order to get it open. At the same time, I was waiting on the Title 4 funding to start at my colleges.

I was mislead so many times with the understanding that I had to do certain things to become accredited in order to get financial aid like a regular four-year university, but man was I wrong. It literally took me more than six years to get financial aid for my college, and we thought it would cover all of the colleges, but again we were wrong. Sitting back thinking about things after I fought so hard to get financial aid, had I moved into my building prematurely, I may not have been able to properly maintain it because the funding wouldn't have been available for the students, which it now was. I would have had to totally depend on the students paying out of their pockets, and in this day and time, that is very difficult. I had all of my stations and furnishings custom built, and it was very exciting. There were major holdups for me pertaining to entering into the building, and I just didn't understand it. Not only was I trying to maintain all of the businesses, but I was living in a building that was brand new but had mold in it because they didn't properly support the water drainage, so now I had to do an emergency move. I so happened to run into a lady who had moved out of her loft in Hyde Park and wanted to rent it. I was like, "Wow! This is amazing."

But she told me I had to move in late at night. I didn't know why until after we got everything moved in. The manager of the building came to my door and said, "Stop moving right now! You are supposed to pay a fee and schedule a move."

I didn't know this, but she knew. She just didn't tell me. Thank God we had moved everything out of the U-Haul before the man came to the door, so we said no problem we will stop moving right this minute. LOL. So, we get in there, and we get settled in finally. The same lady told me that she had a salon downtown and wanted to know if I might be interested in leasing it? So, I'm thinking how crazy would it be for me to lease this new place? I'm already trying to get in my building for the new barber school, and I already don't have enough money to get in there. I was also maintaining my other colleges. What was great about it was that it was a turnkey, so all I had to do was get the key, move in, fill the booths and pay the bills. Considering I was leasing her loft from her to live in, she gave me a break on the salon, so I was actually saving her by agreeing to occupy both spaces. People on the outside looking in probably thought I was balling out of control, and I had it going on. Not knowing how a person is doing and looking at what they are doing can give people the wrong impression. It's best to mind your own business. My main reason for opening up this salon was because I wanted my wife and mother-in-law to have a business they could consider theirs. Also, my wife would understand things that I had to go through, and she would be more understanding as to why I worked so hard for what I believed in. Unfortunately, the salon only lasted for less than a year, but by this time, I had gotten the new barber college open. It was OK. Sometimes businesses work, and sometimes they don't.

My ribbon-cutting ceremony was one of the most exciting things I've ever done, and I was so grateful to God and the people who helped me and stood by my side: my parents, my grandparents, my godmother and the angels that God sent who believed in me. I started analyzing things regarding my marriage, and it just wasn't adding up to me. I busted my butt to be the best husband I could be, no matter what. I made sure I didn't allow my businesses to overtake my marriage with the understanding that my businesses needed to survive in order for me to properly take care of my family.

I sacrificed a lot and digressed tremendously in order to make sure my businesses and my family were taken care of. I was accustomed to getting what I wanted when I wanted it and doing anything I wanted to do. Having a family and responsibilities changes all of those things. I would come home and the lights would be off, and I couldn't figure out what was going on. The bill hadn't been paid and this happened on a number of occasions. Also, my wife's car kept getting repossessed, and I couldn't let them keep it because it would go on her credit and could ruin our future plans, and we would have still had to pay for it. She needed transportation, and we couldn't just rely on one car. I realized no one is perfect and I had my faults as well, but this is when I came to the conclusion that she wasn't good with handling money. We had to come to a happy medium.

I remember we got into an argument once, and I got upset and I kicked a steel garbage can twice into some wood, bent the garbage can, and broke the wood behind it. I almost broke my foot. I did mess up my toe. I didn't know how to deal with the situation with my wife. I felt like she took my meekness for weakness. I didn't have any stress relievers so every now and then I started dealing with other women. I was wrong but I just made sure she didn't find out. I felt horrible because I was cheating and I validated it. How do I help my wife to understand that I was not a punk? One of the ways I would deal with it was to tell her that I was going to the casino once or twice a week, just to get away from her.

She thought I was out gambling, but that wasn't the case all the time. I knew how to play blackjack very well, but I never risked my businesses or anything important to gamble. This was just an excuse to get away from her. I wasn't right by doing it, but I didn't know what else to do. What I didn't want was to seek out other women in order to be happy at home, but I did, and that was a challenge, honestly speaking. I loved my wife so until no matter what, I still maintained a level of respect. She came first under all circumstances, not excluding my daughter. My wife needed a different kind of attention that I willingly gave her. This went on for a while.

I started slipping away from my marriage. You can say I was over it. My wife hated her job, and she had worked there for about ten years. I promised her once everything balanced out, she could move over into my corporation and work with me. That day happened, and I felt like maybe there was another chance for us. I figured, I'm going to get her name tattooed on me to show her I'm not going anywhere, and since she was working for the corporation, we were going to be solid. One day, I went in the school and asked her about my insurance card and she said, "Oh yeah, let me call them and have them send it." I didn't think about it anymore. Some months passed and I asked her about my insurance card again, and she said let me call them and see why they haven't sent it. That same day, about four hours later, I asked her about it again. She said they hadn't emailed her back. Something made me turn around towards her and ask her a question. My question was, "Do I have insurance on my car? Tell me the truth." And her reply was, "I can't lie to you. No, you don't have insurance." And I said, "So I've been riding around for nine months without insurance, and anything could have happened?"

She let the insurance lapse, but she got insurance on her car and left mine without coverage. I asked her do you know how it could have ruined us if I would have had an accident or anything? After this happened, I totally went back to being over her and our marriage.

There are so many more things I could talk about that involves our marriage going sour, but she wasn't in the relationship alone, and it was not about bashing anyone. It was about being open and telling the truth. It also didn't help that someone called her and told her I was cheating on her with another woman. I asked her for details. I wanted to go to the person who I felt said these things, but it never got resolved so I didn't worry about it. Every week, I was spending one or two nights out, so I wouldn't have to be around her. Honestly speaking, I was wrong for doing that, but I felt like I couldn't handle being in the house with her too much. You know, I really loved my wife and I wanted very much for things to work out, but no matter what I did, it just seemed not to. I had my female friends talking to both of us and building a relationship with her and just giving her some words of wisdom, but it just didn't work. At this point, we were toward the end of our marriage, and there was nothing that she could do to change how I felt. I felt violated in so many different ways, and just felt like I wasn't going to deal with anymore nonsense. I wanted out.

We were going through the process of talking divorce,

and I was headed overseas during the divorce proceedings when I got a call that the lights had gotten cut off from the pole at my new barber college while the students were there. My sister, Tramaine, is over all of the budgeting. She was as capable of taking care of those things as I was. We couldn't figure out how this could be. Because my wife worked for the corporation, in the divorce decree I agreed to give her what she was getting paid every week for a period of time whether she found a job or not. Come to find out, she hadn't paid any of the utilities for the salon I had opened downtown the entire time we were there. The electric company cut the lights off at the school so they could collect money for the business that I had closed downtown. In addition, they would not turn the gas on in the new building until I paid the bill in full for the salon. I couldn't believe any of this. The lights stayed off from Tuesday until Friday because I had to wait until they could come back around and turn them back on from the pole. How embarrassing this was, especially when it wasn't even my fault. Who cared? We got the lights back on, and that was all that mattered.

I was in a very, very bitter divorce. Truthfully speaking, I really didn't want to get divorced, but I felt as if I was forced to make the decision based on feeling like I would put my future in jeopardy staying with someone who caused me to get so angry. There was always a lot of tension, so I had to go. I felt like I didn't like her at this point, and no matter what was said about me or done to me, I kept my cool. I didn't publicly display all of my hurt and pain. I just let the inevitable happen. The tattoo that I so affectionately got to prove to her I wasn't going anywhere, I had removed. It was changed to something else, so you can't even tell her name was on my body. LOL. LOL.

God is amazing. Where do I go from here? I was divorced for the third time. I was starting over again. Why was all of these things happening to me? I am a good guy. I really started looking in the mirror at myself, but the good thing about it is I felt like I had an even better opportunity to succeed. My spirit became calm, and I felt like all of my unnecessary problems were going to be over. Problems will always be there, but they wouldn't be problems that I didn't have to encounter. They would be normal problems that came with being a business owner and just living this life. Period. They would not be things that could be prevented!

CHAPTER 12

JUST WHEN I THOUGHT I
WAS DONE GOING THROUGH

Just When I Thought I Was Done Going Through

I finally divorced for the third time, I figured that this was an end to a great beginning, and I wanted to make sure I took advantage of my new start. Little did I know, things started all over again, and it was almost unbelievable. It's really unfortunate when you can't get funding to properly operate your businesses. Being in distress makes you desperate enough to resort to any means necessary. Well, almost anything. I never did anything illegal.

Borrowing money from institutions who charged me 50% interest was the only option I had. Fortunately, they looked at the amount of money my businesses made and figured they couldn't lose, and they were right. The interest added on to my monthly budget was simply outrageous. I couldn't understand what all of this was about. I just didn't get it. Why wouldn't things work out for me? I was doing everything correctly to the best of my ability, and it never ended. I started questioning whether I was really supposed to be doing what I was doing, or should I just quit and give up?

147

That's why it's very important, in my opinion, to get some good sound words to make sure we understand our purpose. The reason the pressure was heightened was because what God had for me, He had to make sure without a doubt I can handle it. I humbly submitted to the call that God placed on my life, and I just continued to work hard and do everything I knew that was right to do. I knew that God had it all under control. For the third time, my marriage didn't work. I really didn't want to be divorced. I couldn't get ahead in my businesses. My biological daughter was in college, and I didn't know which way I was going. I took this time to step back and work on myself to ensure that I wasn't in the way of my dreams being fulfilled. I checked myself in any area that I felt like could stand in my own way. I made sure my attitude was up to par, as far as how I dealt with people and situations. I made sure I wasn't living above my means. Taking care of my personal wants wasn't given precedence over my businesses succeeding.

There were so many good things happening for me, one right after another. Things were looking up, but my finances for some reason didn't match with my status. Wow! How major was that for me to admit. So many people care about status and being showcased, but like the old saying goes, "they don't have a pot to piss in or a window to throw it out of." I couldn't care less about status. I was used to being platformed as early as when I was a toddler when I sat on the organ as my dad played for many great people. I made history by putting the first barber college inside of a county jail in Chicago. I am also grateful to the great sheriffs and directors who worked with me to make this all possible. This was one of my greatest achievements. Why had I even come up with the proposal of putting a barber college inside of a county jail? My reasoning for doing this was probably not something that the average person thinks about. We often stereotype people who don't look like what we think they should look like. We judge the young men and women who have been locked up and write them off as failures. Life, as we see it, is over for them. I did not believe that, and I wanted to make sure I was part of the solution and not the problem. I wanted to do something that would give them hope and a second chance at life. I figured these guys are in jail cutting hair in the barbershops every day. Wouldn't it make sense for them to get credited for their hours of cutting hair? When they get out of prison, they would be able to go right to work, as opposed to getting back out on the streets doing the same things that caused them to get previously locked up. Some might ask, "why not let them simply apply for a 9 to 5 job?"

Since most employers do not want to hire anyone with a criminal background, I suggested barbering as an option. As history tells us, it is the oldest and one of the most important professions in the world, and you can be self-sufficient. As long as you didn't commit a sexual offense, there is a good chance that after you finish school and take your test, you can go before the board, and they will approve you to become licensed. This was one of the most exciting things I've ever done in my life. I wasn't doing this to get a pat on the back. Nor was I doing it because it would get me exposure. It meant more to me that I was helping to give life and hope back to individuals who had fallen by the wayside. I realized that I was no better than they were; I just made different choices. Fact of the matter is, everyone's story is different. You have some people who have never met their fathers. There are individuals who had mothers who were addicted to drugs or alcohol. You had others who grew up drugs being sold or they were given a birthright of being in a gang from their parents.

More than half the jail population doesn't have a high school diploma or GED. I had a program where I even helped them to get a high school diploma. This barber college got a lot of attention from newspapers, radio and, television stations. So many important people wanted to know how it was going. They let me know how wonderful the program was. I remained humble and realized it wasn't about me, but it is about doing my part to help people get another opportunity to be successful in their lives. Some people wondered how I could be in the jail everyday with people they considered to be "hardened criminals." I tell them it's not what they think. Inmates are people just like we are, but they just made the wrong choices. As long as my motive is right, they will recognize it and be welcoming of me inside the facility.

This was all so unbelievable to me. I even have my own office inside the jail. Through God all things are possible, I thought. What made this program so significant was that because I own barber colleges outside of the jail, if people didn't complete their hours while they were incarcerated, I could transfer their hours and they could finish up in one of

Larry's Barber Colleges on the outside. Another major part of this program was that my instructors and I go to court with the inmates and write letters to judges to help with the decision on whether they should get out or have reduced sentences. What a wonderful feeling knowing that a judge would let me get up and speak on behalf of these inmates and discuss the barber program and how it would help them get out and not be a repeat offender.

In the back of my mind, I'm thinking all of this is great and I'm doing all of this free of charge because no amount of money could compare to the lives that are being changed. All I wanted to do is just succeed in my businesses. Was that too much to ask for? The important thing was that I continued to do everything I knew to do and not waiver based on what I was dealing with. I just had to keep working hard, and I did. As time went on, I was blessed to be connected to a young man who wanted to start a barber college and this afforded me the opportunity to obtain another location, which made a total of three Larry's Barber Colleges. It amazed me that when I thought nothing was changing in certain areas, this came about. I was honored and thrilled at the same time.

CHAPTER 13

WHAT'S THE HOLD UP?
WHY IS IT TAKING ME SO LONG TO GET AHEAD?

153

I was trying to figure out what was really going on and how was all of this supposed to work? I continued to do everything that I was supposed to do, but I still hadn't gotten to where I'm trying to go? Things weren't where I would like for them to have been, but they were definitely not where they used to be. I have never been so structured and organized with my businesses. I didn't understand what the holdup was for me to just feel as though all of my financial struggles were over. My corporation has gotten rather large, and my staff has grown to more people than I'd ever had during my 21 years in business. My sister serves as the director of the colleges and is the CFO, so she does all of the budgeting and has been in this position now for eight years. Normally it's difficult to work with family, especially with my sister being spoiled, but she and I had a good talk and we learned how to work through any problems that might arise. What was important was to make sure the businesses succeed so that we could pass on the legacy. Also, we had to make sure that all the young men and women—and not just limited to just the young—could be successful and reach their goals quicker and smoother than I had. One of the best things about LSE Enterprises, Inc. (Larry's Barber Colleges) is that we take pride in what we do. As easy as it sounds, it;s very difficult. With Title 4 funding, there are lots of extra rules and regulations you have to abide by. Having to adhere to them isn't the problem for us, but making sure that the rest of the staff and the students are doing their part is the most challenging aspect. Once we got the hang of everything, the process went great, until some people who had false credentials did some work for us that caused us to be subjected to a visit from our accreditation company and the Department Of Education.

Getting approval for the other colleges to receive Title 4 funding was prolonged, and it didn't seem fair. How could this be? The most important lesson I learned in this situation was as long as I continue doing everything I know is right, no matter what said or done, victory shall me mine. The craziest thing in the world was that throughout this entire malfunction with the setback with the colleges, I know it wasn't because I had purposely done anything wrong. I was assured that this was just another test that would make my testimony stronger. As many times that I have been through storms, God always brought me out. So, why wouldn't he bring me out of this storm? The most important thing was how you dealt with going through your trial that would determined how you come out. I never changed who I was under any circumstances. Of course, we all have our good days and our bad days. Despite all of that, I remained faithful to my call.

My call was being a father, business owner, leader, friend, musician, and example for others, while I remained focused. We all waiver, but I believe I was built on solid ground, so I always stood tall. I don't judge anyone for who they are or how they decided to conduct their lives. I am responsible for Larry. I would often think about other ways to escape the pressures of life and whether these things could help make things better. Would drinking take my problems away? Would getting high using drugs take my problems away? Would cursing out everyone who upset me or did me wrong take my problems away? Would having sex with multiple women take my problems away? Actually, NONE OF THE ABOVE. All of these temporary fixes would just compound the existing problems.

I have a lot of integrity and am not prideful at all. It is very important that I maintain high standards both inside and outside of my businesses. I often thought about throwing in the towel with my businesses because I felt like if I had to give in to what I know is wrong, then I'd prefer not to even be in business. Realizing that there are too many lives at stake and destinies who are connected to mine, I couldn't give up under any circumstance. I strive very hard to make sure I do what I need to do so that no one has to pay for my mistakes.

Larry's Barber Colleges are really "Educating A New Generation Of Barbers." We have to stand our grounds as to what is right. When students enter into our colleges we have to teach them how to be professionals. Some of the young men and women don't understand how different things could make or break their careers. You can't set your salon or barbershop up where you are only catering to one genre of people. You have to make sure it's suitable and respectable for everyone. With all of this said, this is why I incorporated a life coach class with mentoring, along with the other daily classes. Contrary to popular belief, some people can't move forward if they haven't dealt with certain issues that could stand in their way. There are young men and women who truly do not understand the morals and values of life. They simply can't be productive if these two things are missing. Holding on to our standards means that I can't allow students to come to school and do what they want to do because it would defeat the purpose of teaching them how to be successful in not only this industry, but most importantly, in life.

We have a Larry's Barber College shuttle bus. We are currently working on Larry's Barber College campuses where students would be able to live while attending school. We have smartboards in some of the classrooms to create a more technology-driven teaching environment.

I never thought in a million years that I would be at this place in my life. It feels like I started from the bottom, but now I'm here. When I look back over the years, it amazes me how far I've come. I realize that it could only be God. I'm not where I would like to be right now, but I'm definitely not where I used to be. For that I'm very thankful. Everything is peaceful for me, and I've reflected on many areas of my business to make sure that I was in no way jeopardizing my businesses. I didn't obtain a car with a car note, nor did I buy another house where I had to pay a mortgage. I didn't incur any personal bills that would cause me to have to depend on my businesses to survive. At this point, I believe I got it, and I feel like I'm ready and prepared for everything that God has in store for me. This makes me more excited to continue pressing forward. I've been working hard and diligently and I've learned how to handle all of my situations, whether business or personal, very gracefully. I help people. I treat people well, despite what my needs are or what I am going through. I know it's my time. I've continued traveling the world touring, playing music, and also working on major things in the barber industry. What more could I ask for at this point?

Anyone who knows me, knows that I wake up very early in the morning. I believe I get up before the roosters. LOL. I start my journey for the day. I consider myself pretty structured and disciplined. I think I'm very consistent with my routine, and it's important for me because I have too many things going on not to be. One particular Tuesday morning, I got up early but decided I wasn't going to leave out the house as early as I normally would. I lived in Hyde Park, and I was upstairs in my loft and heard a knock on the door at around 9:30 a.m.,but I didn't pay it any attention because I figured the knocking was at someone else's door. Then I heard several more knocks, which caused me to get up to see what was going on. I looked out the peephole and saw five sheriffs at the door, so I opened it, not knowing what was going on.

"You heard us knocking on the door?" one guy asked.

I looked at another sheriff, and he had a battering ram. I'm thinking to myself, "What is happening?"

Little did I know I was being evicted from the apartment I was renting from someone else.

A couple of the officers were like, "Wait a minute! I know you. Aren't you Larry from the barber colleges?"

"Yes, I am. What is going on? I asked.

"Man, we are sorry, but we have a court order to put whoever is in this apartment out, so you have to put your clothes on and leave, the sheriff said.

By this time, it seemed like this was all a joke because I couldn't possibly be getting evicted from the place I live. This has never happened before in my life. I asked if I could get in the shower and get myself together. "Nope. You just have to get your clothes on and leave. The people from the bank are out in the hall, and you can make arrangements with them." WOW!!!!! Is this really happening to me right now? The sheriffs who knew me understood what was happening, but at this point, there was nothing they could do. I put on some clothes without brushing my teeth or showering. I signed the paperwork they had for me. They took pictures of my apartment and everything I had in there, and basically, said OK. Now you have to leave. Mind you, I was leaving behind more than 300 pairs of shoes, closets and shelves full of clothes, 250 bottles of expensive cologne, a bunch of jewelry, about fifty pairs of designer eyeglasses, furniture, dishes, coats, televisions, musical equipment, computers, and all of my business papers and files, I was really in disbelief at this point because I had no idea how

I was going to get my things. I went out in the hallway, and I expected a banker with a suit and a tie on. I saw three Hispanic guys with a drill and locks to change all of the locks on the doors. I asked them what I needed to do in order to get my things, and they were very nice about telling me. I was very appreciative of this because they could have acted nasty towards me. By this time, the sheriffs had left, and the guys allowed me to come back into the apartment and gather what I needed for right now. I could call a number they gave me to retrieve all the rest of my things at a later date. That was a relief to me. I went back in and a took one of my big duffle bags and grabbed all my jewelry, titles to all my cars and any other important papers I could carry, along with my laptop. What else could I get? It was only me, and they were just letting me grab a few things. I told them thank you went downstairs to the garage got in my car. I sat there not believing this was happening, but also trying to figure out WHERE WAS I GOING TO GO. I HAD NO CLUE. I called the people from the bank first to see what I needed to do in order to get my things, and I had to produce documents showing them that I lived there and luckily, I had some of the papers in the car that stated I lived there. After I called them, I thought about where I could go at the last minute. I needed to be where I wouldn't inconvenience anyone and where I could be comfortable and have peace of mind until I found another place to live. I called my grandparents and explained to them what happened, and they told me to come out to their house until I got myself together. But then I didn't' have any clothes. I only had the clothes on my back and the shoes on my feet. I had no underwear, no toiletries. Half way to my grandparents house, and I got an idea. "I'm the best customer at the cleaners because I always have the most clothes, so I have clothes in the cleaners." I got off the expressway and went back down to my cleaners, and thankfully, I was right. I had a load of clothes there, which they allowed me to take without paying because they loved me so much. I headed back out towards my grandparents' house, even though I hated the suburbs, but knowing I can't be choosy in this case. I had to go where I could lay my head with no problem. Prior to arriving at my grandparents house, I stopped off and purchased things that were necessary for me to at least shower brush my teeth and an extra pair of gym shoes to wear. I had on some green Cole Haans that I definitely couldn't wear with every outfit. LOL.

I arrived at my grandparents house and I explained to them what had happen and that it was really beyond my control. The lady I was renting from basically had been stringing me along. She actually lost her condo to foreclosure. I never used the mailbox because the management company wasn't aware that she was renting the apartment to me for the past few years. I used a P.O. Box and my business addresses for my mail, which was OK with me. The bank called the management company to see if anyone lived in the apartment, and they told them no, because they didn't think anyone was living there. The association dues weren't even being paid. They didn't know to contact me, so without a way to give me any notice, the bank was allowed to come and take over the apartment, which I could have stopped had I known about it. My grandparents told me to stay there as long as I needed to stay, and I was very grateful, but I told them I would only stay until I found a place to live.

Two weeks had gone by and I finally had gotten a call from the bank telling me that I could set a date to go and retrieve my things, which I was very happy to be able to do. I really didn't have any place to put all of my furniture and things, so I just gave everything away to anyone who wanted or needed it. I called people and gave away a lot of shoes and clothes, just so it wouldn't be cluttered at my grandparents' house because I definitely wasn't putting any of my things in storage. I rented a U-Haul truck and was able to get all of my things out of the condo. I got back to the house and stored all of my things neatly in the basement and in my room. Now, I was all set. To think that I was a successful businessman who was forty years old, and I was living with my grandparents. "WHAT IS REALLY GOING ON?" I remained humble and thankful for even being able to have a place to live where I was comfortable. Their home was very neat and clean, and there were no problems there. I would have gone to my parents' home, but there was no room for me there. It would have never worked out, and I didn't want to be a burden on anyone at all.

A few weeks went by, and I was chilling comfortably living with my grandparents until I got my new place, when I got a call at work one day from my grandmother saying my dad had fallen down the stairs. I called my dad's phone. No answer. I called my mom, and she said she hadn't heard anything. I called my sister and she didn't know what was going on, either. My dad then called me back and said "Wassup, Larry? I was doing a funeral?" It was actually my grandfather who had fallen down the stairs and hit his head. This happened because he needed to have a surgery for the past fifteen years, but he was afraid to have it because he didn't want to lose his ability to walk. My grandmother had a stroke in 2004. She's had multiple knee surgeries, and she is on a walker. My grandfather was the main caregiver for both of them. He cooked, washed, cleaned, and drove them wherever they needed to go. Now he was out of commission in the hospital preparing for this surgery, which meant that everything fell on me. I had to think about why I was put in the position at this particular time as I was moving in with my grandparents. I would be there to make sure my grandmother was taken care of, and I could help my grandfather recover after his surgery. God makes no mistakes, and everything happens for a reason. The doctor told my grandfather that he couldn't lift more than five pounds for a while, so I made sure that all of my grandparents' needs were met to the best of my ability. When the winter approached, I asked my grandparents how much longer they needed me to stay, and my grandfather's reply was, "Well, I can't lift more than five pounds for at least another month or two."

My grandmother said, "We don't want you to go. Stay here as long as you want and save your money." By this time, I'm thinking, is this really happening? Being with my grandparents gave me one of the biggest joys of my life because they have been married for close to sixty years, and their relationship is amazing. Seeing the way my grandfather took care of my grandmother showed me where my dad learned how to care for my mother. I learned it from my dad, so it encouraged me more to never give up on marriage and to be a strong, responsible man at the end of the day. Take care of your family by any positive means necessary.

Now what? I'm living with the grandparents and running my businesses. I have no major personal bills, so things aren't as bad as they may have seemed. Recently, I've done a lot of traveling for business purposes, and I've been even more focused on things that are necessary to continue my journey. I'm not so quick to make any decisions without making sure that it would be beneficial for me, my family, and my businesses.

I used to think that not living anymore would make everything go away, but I was wrong because it would have hurt so many people. Also, so many people would have not had a chance to be connected to my destiny had I not lived. I do everything I do from a genuine place with no negative motives at all. I've had just about everything I've ever desired. So it's not about acquiring material things, but I strive to be successful and rich to create more opportunities for those who seek them.

This has been a wonderful journey, and honestly, I wouldn't trade it for the world. Life has its ups and downs, but again, you have to know your purpose and how you deal with what you go through. That will determine how you come out. It's not over yet. I'm working on putting Larry's Barber Colleges all over the world and also in as many correctional institutions as possible. I will continue to keep my standards lifted and teach what's right as well as do what is right. I will maintain integrity and walk with dignity.

Stay tuned for the next episode of my life. My life is worth living, and so is yours. Suicide Is Not The Answer but a good healthy life is.

We don't want to commit suicide in our hearts in any shape, form, or fashion. Wanting to commit suicide is merely a cry for attention. We are really saying, we are hurting, and we need someone to listen and talk to us. We often wear these smiles on our faces, yet we are unhappy. It's hard for people who think they know you to believe it. Suicide Is Not The Answer. God can't forgive you for something you can't ask to be forgiven for. Besides, I would have missed out on all of the great years I have ahead of me. I have a wonderful family who I know loves me very much, and I love them just as much. It is better to be rich in family and love than to be rich in money. Money can't make you happy if you are not happy within.

If you have some unfinished business that you need to deal with, deal with it from a positive standpoint. Face it, destroy it, and then bury it so it won't continue to wreak havoc in your life and bury you. Things are already lookin' betta for me.

Much love, Larry